Establishing the Reign of Natural Liberty:

A Common Law Training Manual

Issued by the International Common Law Court of Justice

March 1, 2017

Table of Contents

Preface	3
Philosophy	3
Humanity and Consciousness	4
Natural Law Basis of Common Law	5
The Common Law and its Courts	10
How Do We Use the Common Law?	13
Matters before a Common Law Court	14
Establishing and Maintaining the Court	19
Legal Procedure and Court Protocol	22
Convictions and Verdicts	31
Enforcement	33
Sheriffs and Peace Officers	37
On Citizens' Arrests	42
Consequences: A World made New	44
Appendix 1: Sovereign Basis of the Court	47
Appendix 2: The Peoples' Assemblies	49
Appendix 3: Purpose and Nature of our Struggle	57
Appendix 4: Common Law Court Documents	70
Appendix 5: ITCCS Program	73
Appendix 6: Art and Rules of War	74
Appendix 7: Kevin Annett Biography	82
Sources and Resources	85
Post script	104

This Manual provides instruction and training to those who have moved from words to actions. We speak to people who not only recognize the permanent war being waged against humanity by a global corporate tyranny, but who are actively dismantling that murderous system at its source so that justice can be made real in a reclaimed world.

You are part of a growing movement to create a new, liberated society within the shell of the old by first allowing the law to act for all people and not just the wealthy and their clique of judicial specialists. That new society is emerging through every act of courage and integrity by we who know that our children and the future of humanity are at stake.

Let us be guided in our efforts by Aristotle's First Principle of Reason: that one must understand the nature of any phenomenon or system to predict its actions and outcome.

The Three Universal Axioms of Natural Law

Unity of Creation: The nature and power of all creation is contained within every one of its elements. All things take their substance from the nature of the whole, and every element of that whole is equal to every other element. This unity is the basis for the harmony and commonality of all things.

Commonality of Creation: As a consequence of this unity, every part of creation is connected to and mutually dependent on every other part. By nature, things that are equal to the same common source are equal to each other. Therefore, all things are by that nature placed in common and every part has an equal share in creation.

Goodness of Creation: The Natural Law establishes the wholeness and integrity of all parts of creation. Energy and life is kept in a continual balance for the health and growth of every part. Reality is infused with a divine balance and harmony.

Humanity and its Sovereign, Self-Governing Consciousness

Men and women are a complete creation dependent on nothing but their own nature, which endows them with an inherent self-governance: that is, the desire and capacity to be fully responsible for themselves, others and creation. This nature is expressed through their reason and virtue, which are infused with and manifest all three of the natural laws.

The inborn reason and virtue of people express these laws and manifest as just moral and political principles of Liberty, Equality and Peace. People are capable of living according to these laws through their own sovereign consciousness which makes them just, self-governing men and women who can form lasting covenants by which to live.

This sovereign consciousness directs random events into virtuous, purposeful action according to the Natural Law and thereby creates ethical existence and meaning. As a mirror of creation, it is human nature to be self-governing, to seek what is right and just for all people, to avoid enmity and warfare, and to share the fruits of creation and their labor with all people.

Natural Law is the Basis of Common Law

What we call the Common Law arises from the normal interaction of people with one another according to their nature and customs, which maintain peace and equity between themselves. This Common Law is the human manifestation of the universal Natural Law, and creates no hierarchy or dominating force over people. On the contrary, common law engenders and defends the natural liberty and just equality of all people without regard to rank or distinction.

The root of the common law lies in the Anglo-Saxon tribal traditions of Europe and their village-based system of justice and government. In this tradition, authority arose from the will of the people and not a ruler, since liberty was understood to dwell inherently within every man and woman born. Rights are not granted by one person to another, since they exist *"ab initio"*: from the beginning. All people therefore have the inborn capacity to govern themselves, to know right from wrong and act justly, and to judge for themselves all things, including the conduct of others.

This inborn capacity rather than imposed statute was the tribal guarantee of social peace and harmony. But alongside this common law arose a contrary system of governance derived from state-level Empires and their religions that saw people not as inherently free but rather as chattels and property of others. This imperial system of domination has always been at permanent war with the liberty and equality of the common law.

We summarize this Natural Liberty and the basis of Common Law as follows:

1. Every man, woman and child is born and is by nature free, equal and sovereign, and possesses an inherent knowledge of what is true and right. Accordingly, no-one can be subordinated to another or to any external authority, since every person's inherent wisdom and liberty makes them

complete and sufficient creations in themselves, within a wider community of equals.

2. This personal sovereignty is a reflection of the wider Natural Law, whereby all life by nature is indivisible and placed in common for the survival and happiness of all. In any just society, this commonality endows all people with the unalienable right to establish among themselves their own governance, and defend themselves against any tyranny or violence, including that inflicted by external authorities. Any authority that rules unjustly and arbitrarily, without the free and uncoerced consent of the people, has lost its right to rule and can be lawfully overthrown - *Unjust government is not government but tyranny - Plato*

3. This Natural Law gives rise to customary Common Law whose purpose is to protect the inherent liberties and sovereignty of men and women in a community by maintaining equity and peace among them. The Common Law derives its authority from the people themselves, and from the capacity of the people to know what is just and to judge right and wrong for themselves. This capacity is expressed in a jury system of twelve freely chosen people who are the ultimate judge and authority in Common Law courts.

4. Historically, Common Law and its early expression in the Magna Carta of 1215 arose in England after the 11th century Norman Conquest as a bulwark of defense of the people against the arbitrary rule of self-appointed elites like monarchs and popes. The authority of these elites was derived unnaturally, from warfare, conquest and the theft of the earth, rather than from the consent of the community and its basis, the divine law of peace and equality. This elite rule arose most strongly in the Roman Empire and its descendent, the Church of Rome, according to whose beliefs God is a

dominator and conqueror (*domine*), and all people are subjects of the Pope.

5. Such a conquest-based rule of papal and kingly elites gave rise to a legal system known as Civil or Roman Law, and the belief that men and women are not endowed with the capacity for self-rule and wisdom. All law and authority is therefore derived externally, from statutes devised and imposed by a ruler, whether a pope, a monarch or a government. This system developed from Aristotelian philosophy and Roman property law in which creation is divided and human beings are treated as chattels and the possessions of others, and are thereby devoid of inherent liberties. **The people are thus in every sense enslaved, cut off from the world given freely and in common to all. This slave system ranks and categorizes all people, and grants restricted "freedoms" (friethoms or slave privileges) that are defined and limited through statutes issued by rulers.**

6. Common and Civil (Roman) Law are therefore fundamentally opposed and are at war with each other. They cannot be reconciled, since they arise from two completely different notions of humanity and justice: Common Law knows life as a free gift given equally to all, while under Civil Law, life is a conditional privilege, and humanity is a managed slave populace. Accordingly, governments operate in practice according to Civil (statute) law and denigrate or ignore Common Law altogether through the rule of unaccountable judge-dominated courts.

7. The most extreme form of elite-based Civil/Roman Law is what is called Papal or Canon Law, which defines the Church of Rome as the only legitimate authority on earth to which all other laws, people and governments are subordinate. Canon law is self-governing and completely unaccountable to

anything but itself. Behind its front of Christian rhetoric, Roman Catholicism is a neo-pagan cult based upon the late 3rd century Roman Emperor-worship system known as Sol Invictus, in which one sovereign entitled God and Master (*Deus et Dominus*) rules heaven and earth: formally the Emperor and now the Pope. This tyrannical cult has not surprisingly been the cause of more warfare, genocide, conquest and murder than any power in human history, and continues to constitute the single greatest threat to Common Law and human liberty.

8. The Church of Rome was the first and is the oldest corporation on our planet: a legal entity designed for the protection of tyrants, which nullifies the individual liability and responsibility of the elites for any crime or conquest they perpetrate. From Rome and the Vatican Incorporated has spread the contagion that now threatens to destroy our planet and our lives, as unaccountable corporate oligarchy everywhere subverts liberty and the health of our planet by subordinating all of life to profit and power.

9. At this very moment of corporate conquest and its subjugation of humanity, a counter-movement is arising to reassert the divine purpose and its operation through the Common Law, and to restore the earth and humanity to their natural being as a common body. This movement is foretold biblically and in prophecy as the time when all people are returned to their natural equality, devoid of all divisions, privileges and oppression, in order live in harmony with creation and one another.

10. This restoration of humanity to its natural condition of freedom and equality is a divine purpose. It begins by actively dis-establishing all existing authority and institutions derived

from Roman civil law, and replacing them with a new governance under Common Law jurisdiction. The creation of that new Natural Law authority among a liberated humanity is the fundamental purpose of the Common Law Courts.

The way to secure liberty is to place it in the peoples' hands, that is, to give them the power at all times to defend it in the legislature and in the courts of justice.

- John Adams, 1798

Establishing the Reign of Natural Liberty: The Common Law and its Courts

What is assembling is the first court in history to bring judgment against the Vatican and the Crown of England as institutions. But our Court also signals the dawn of a new notion of justice: one defined by the people themselves, and especially by the historic victims of church and state, to bring about not only a judgment on their persecutors, but a new political and spiritual arrangement to undo the systems responsible for inter generational crimes against humanity. - from the founding Charter of The International Common Law Court of Justice, September 1, 2012

History was made on February 11, 2013, when the first Catholic Pope in history resigned from his office during peacetime in order to avoid arrest for protecting and aiding child raping and trafficking priests.

Barely two weeks later, the same Pope Benedict, Joseph Ratzinger, was found guilty by the International Common Law Court of Justice for Crimes against Humanity , including child trafficking. And the universal Arrest Warrant that he had anticipated and provoked his resignation was issued against him on February 25.

Evading justice inside the Vatican, Ratzinger is an international fugitive from the law, and a living example of the power of Courts of justice to reclaim the law from the wealthy and their compliant governments. *(see www.itccs.org)*

"Man is born free, but everywhere he is in chains." That fact has altered little over the centuries. But the chains of oppression over much of our species have been forged through the weapons of violence and ignorance, and they can be undone.

Long before any rulers held sway over humanity, men and women established customs and laws among themselves to ensure their peace and liberties as free, self-governing people. They did so from an inherent recognition of a Natural Law of Equality or Divine Law whereby no one has any right to dominate or rule over others, to seize more of creation than another, or to own any part of a world given equally to all people.

It is the Principle of Creation that every child born is endowed with unalienable liberties that no authority, law, government or religion can diminish or abolish. Any power that attempts to do so is tyrannical and illegitimate, even if it operates according to its own laws – for such tyranny is a denial of the natural order and an attack upon divinity and humanity.

These three great social principles emerge from such Natural Law:

1. **All things exist and are held in common.** By the state of nature, no one has any more of a claim to the earth and its wealth than another, as noted by a founder of modern law, Thomas Hobbes: *I demonstrate in the first place, that in the natural state of men (which state we may properly call the state of nature) all men have equal right to all things.* (Leviathan, 1651)

2. **By extension, no-one has any natural authority over another.** In the words of Jean-Jacques Rousseau in The Social Contract (1762), "Since no man has a natural authority over his fellow, and force creates no right, we must conclude that covenants form the basis of all legitimate authority among men."

3. **The Law does harm to no-one.** (*Actus Regis Nemini Facit Injuriam*) Arising from the Natural Law of equity and harmony, no-one can lawfully harm another, and if one does no harm to another he cannot be guilty of any offense. John Stuart Mill articulated this principle in his work On Liberty where he argued that, the only purpose for which power can be rightfully exercised over any member of a civilized community, against its will is to prevent harm to others. (1869)

An equivalent idea was earlier stated in France's Declaration of the Rights of Man and of the Citizen of 1789 as, "Liberty consists in the freedom to do everything which injures no one else; hence the exercise of the natural rights of each man has no limits except those which assure to the other members of the society the enjoyment of the same rights. These limits can only be determined by law."

This Natural Law exists to maintain the natural peace and equity between people and is their shield and protector against unjust rule, rather than a force over them. Within the ancient traditions of tribal communities, especially in the Anglo-Saxon world, this Law evolved into what became known as the Customary or Common Law, or the Law of the Land or Nature. It has strong echoes in the customs of indigenous nations all over the world.

How Do We Use the Common Law?

The truth is that throughout everyday life, people everywhere use and rely on Common Law to live and work together. It is simply the inherent way that people conduct their affairs. Liken it to the roots that bind together human communities by unconditionally upholding the life, dignity and well being of every man, woman and child. These roots are foundational and become especially necessary in the face of tyrannical powers.

The Common Law's firm horizontal guarantees of mutual respect and protection are a permanent threat to the efforts by arbitrary rulers to harness men and women into the unnatural and vertical arrangement known as the State. That is why every government and religion seeks to annul the Common Law with their own authority and statutes, in order to reduce free peoples everywhere to the status of regimented, obedient tax-paying wage slaves who serve a ruling clique.

To extend our everyday reign of Common Law into all areas of life means to challenge the arbitrary rule of those cliques, and of all State level regimes. But the very fact that Common Law serves we, the vast majority of humanity, means that it only needs to be consistently practiced by us for autocracies and oppression to crumble.

We use the Common Law by simply employing and relying on it, in all spheres of life. And that means by establishing Common Law Courts of record with absolute jurisdiction over our lives and communities.

Matters before a Common Law Court

Traditionally, law in the European tradition falls into two general categories: civil and criminal law. The former deals with disputes between individuals – often called "Tort" offenses – or issues of negligence which cause harm. Criminal law deals with acts of intentional harm to individuals but which, in a larger sense, are offenses against all people because they somehow threaten the community.

Arising as a defense against absolutism and state or church tyranny, the Common Law traditionally has dealt with Criminal Law matters that crown or canon law courts refuse either to address, or do so in a restricted manner, including murder, rape, warfare and other crimes against the community. But civil matters of personal disputes may also be brought into a Common Law Court, which after all claims universal jurisdiction over all legal matters within a community. Indeed, because Common Law is rooted in the jury system, what better forum can there be for the settling of civil matters between individuals than a trial before one's own neighbors?

For our purposes, however, the major focus of litigation before our Common Law Courts will be on Criminal Law and matters involving serious threats or crimes made against people, animals, communities, and the environment.

As in any lawful system, the burden of proof in any such litigation brought before the Common Law Court will be on the plaintiffs – those bringing the lawsuit – and normal Rules of Evidence will apply. For example, allegations against a party cannot be made in court without there being a basis in provable facts, such as primary documentation that is certified by an independent party, or by producing eyewitnesses to the alleged crime.

Another crucial Rule of Evidence is the inadmissibility of hearsay evidence, as in "no, I wasn't there, but I *heard.*" This is an especially relevant rule when it comes to the commission of serious crimes such as genocide, murder or rape.

In short, any allegation must be backed up with provable facts, and must be made by one who was a direct participant in or an eyewitness to the event.

For our purposes, it must be noted that in the case of especially monstrous, corporate crimes committed by governments or other powers, such as wars of aggression, genocide or human trafficking, normal rules of evidence are less stringently applied. This is because of a realistic understanding that crimes committed by entire societies or regimes are of a different nature than crimes by isolated individuals. A different set of norms regarding intent and provable evidence applies.

In the words of the American prosecutor at the Nuremberg Trials in 1946, Robert Jackson:

"No regime that seeks the extermination of entire groups of people generally retains written proof of their intent to commit this crime. Considering the murderous nature of their regime, there is no need, since such extermination is not considered a crime. Nevertheless, even such a system seeks to fog and dissimulate the evidence, especially during wartime. The proof of crimes against humanity generally lies not in documents but in the witness of survivors, in mass graves, and *in the implied proof of the intent to commit these crimes contained in the everyday and institutionalized laws, attitudes and norms of the murderous regime.*"

Implied intent is a legal concept especially relevant and specific to litigation involving genocidal regimes, including governments and churches whose world view and laws consider other groups to be unworthy of life or equal rights, such as the churches and states that were tried and sentenced in the first case of the International Common Law Court of Justice concerning the genocide of indigenous peoples in Canada. (*www.itccs.org* , *www.murderbydecree.com*)

Laws such as the Indian Act of Canada, which impose a different set of laws on a racially targeted group, or the Roman Catholic *Crimen Sollicitationas*, which condones and facilitates the concealment of child rape within the church, indicate a clear implied intent to commit and abet criminal acts.

That is, it is unnecessary to prove the individual intent to harm children by Catholic priests, since under their own self-governing rules called Canon Law, every priest is systematically required to harm children by aiding those who do so if he is to retain his job and ordination. The *collective guilt* of these clergy as a whole is implied and clear, just as it was concerning all of the servants of the Nazi regime.

Thus, while normal due process requires that the prosecution prove that the accused committed an act and did so with deliberate intent, such an intent may also be assumed to exist by the larger context of a crime, especially when that crime is perpetrated by entire organizations or regimes.

Ascertaining the truth is always laborious, but ultimately the process is best guaranteed by a body of jurors than single adjudicators. Common law juries and not individual judges are a better guard against the abuse of Rules of Evidence and just procedure in a courtroom.

Self-governing judges are notoriously prone to corruption and political manipulation, and when appointed by the very governments under criminal investigation, are obviously unsuited to the task of rendering a fair judgment. In fact, under legal procedure, such state-appointed judges have no jurisdictional competence to rule on the criminality and guilt of their employers. Judges routinely waive just procedure and rules of evidence, and are authorized to do so by statute law. In Canada, "crown" appointed judges even have the power to alter or destroy court records, silence one party in a dispute, and ignore due process altogether!

The whole point of establishing a jury-run Common Law Court is to prevent such a manipulation of the law and justice by unaccountable parties or vested interests. It is not accidental that a Founding Father of the American Republic, John Hancock, said in 1777,

"If we have not Courts that are established and maintained by the People, rather than by corruptible Judges, then we will have no Republic. Our Constitution and our Nation will rise or fall according to the independence of our Courts."

Canada and its churches, along with their sponsors in London and Rome, committed a deliberate and massive campaign of genocide against aboriginal children for over a century.

Under International law such a criminal regime has lost its right to govern or expect allegiance from its citizens.

From the verdict of the International Common Law Court of Justice Brussels

February 25, 2013

Establishing and Maintaining Common Law Courts

The Common Law's First Principles establish its general legitimacy and lawfulness. This valid system gives rise to Courts with the power to protect the people as a whole by prosecuting and indicting any persons and institutions that threaten the community.

The mandate to establish such Courts is derived from the sovereignty of the people as a whole, and not from any particular political system or government. Common Law Courts are therefore *universal*, not constricted by customary borders or laws, and possess the jurisdictional competence to adjudicate any issue or grievance. Common Law Courts are not subject to and do not recognize any other legal or political authority, immunity or privilege, like those routinely claimed by heads of churches and states.

Enjoying universal jurisdiction because of its rootedness in the Natural Law, Common Law Courts can be established in any country or community, and not only within nations with a specifically common law legal tradition, such as England, Canada and America.

Common Law Courts are established when any number of men and women come together to judge a matter of concern to them and to their community. Political protests, "town hall gatherings" or Tribunals of Conscience that unite citizens and give voice to their concerns are often the first step. Common Law courts are an expression of that voice.

The Court itself is established by the direct will and vote of the people as a whole, who gather in assembly and elect a citizen Jury of at least twelve people. They also appoint a Citizen Prosecutor to conduct the case if needed, a presiding Adjudicator whose job is strictly advisory, and a Sheriff and group of Peace Officers to enforce the summonses, warrants and verdicts of the Court. Additionally, the community may appoint local magistrates versed in the law known as Justices of the Peace (JP's), who traditionally have the power to summon juries and issue warrants. The JP or a local Sheriff may also initiate a Common Law court. *("**The Sovereign Basis of Common Law Courts**", **Appendix 1**)*

All of the participants in a Common Law Court must present their own case in all of the Court proceedings, since to allow another to "re-present" them would constitute a surrender of their natural rights and sovereignty. This applies both to the plaintiffs and the defendants involved in any matter before the Court. There are, accordingly, no professional lawyers or permanent presiding judges in a Common Law Court system.

There is no restriction on the power of a Common Law Court to access any person, place or thing, nor any limitation on the duration or rights of the Court. The Court and its Magistrate can issue Public Summonses that are binding on any person or institution, and enforceable by the Court Sheriff, who has an unrestricted right to detain any person named in the Summons and bring them into Court.

The final verdict of the Common Law Court Jury is final and not subject to appeal, simply because a reasonable and non-coerced group of citizens can come to the truth of any matter on the basis of the evidence alone, possessed as they are of an inherent knowledge of right and wrong. The truth is not mutable. A defendant is either innocent or guilty; the truth is not subject to revision or reconsideration, since then it is not true.

However, if it can be proven beyond any doubt that the Court's verdict was made unlawfully, was unduly influenced, or occurred on the basis of incomplete or faulty evidence, a Common Law Magistrate can re-open and re-try the case with the normal Jury and Court officers.

In the same way, the sentence of the Court is also final, and is enforced not only by the Court Sheriff but by all citizens. For the Common Law arises from and is the direct responsibility of all people, as are all of its procedures. The verdict really is a declaration of the people that they will govern themselves according to their own democratic law and decisions.

Finally, upon issuing its final verdict and sentence, the Common Law Court jury is automatically concluded and its members are released from their duty. No Court is maintained without the conscious consent and participation of the people themselves.

Again, there is no professional, permanent caste of either lawyers or judges in a Common Law Court system, but rather elected and temporary Court officers.

Legal Procedure and Court Protocol

Common Law, being derived from Natural Justice, bases its legal procedures on the centrality of *Due Process*: the three-fold right of anyone to be notified of the charges being brought against him, to see the evidence in such a suit, and to be tried and judged before his own peers. No legitimate trial can proceed nor can a conviction be rendered if the accused has not been given these rights, and afforded the chance to freely defend himself in a court of law.

Such rights are based on these fundamental doctrines of the Common Law:

1. It is presumed that the accused is innocent, not guilty;
2. The burden of proof of the accused's guilt rests not upon the defendant but the plaintiff, who must convince a jury of the guilt of the accused beyond any reasonable doubt, and
3. The accused cannot be detained without due process but must appear promptly before a Court, according to the principle of *Habeas Corpus*, which is Latin for "produce the body."

Both sides in a dispute are given equal time to file their statements and evidence, make motions to the Court, and respond to arguments. But to avoid "vexatious litigation" designed to simply harass or disrupt an adversary – which can drag out and impede justice and due process itself – the Court normally sets a strict time limit on pre-trial proceedings, after which the trial commences.

The pre-trial period allows both sides to present their evidence and arguments to one another in order to seek a settlement prior to a Court appearance. This presentation is usually referred to as Examination for Discovery or Voir Dire ("to see and say") where either party can demand any relevant evidence or document from the other. If Examination does not produce a settlement of differences, then the Court is convened and a trial begins.

The general procedures and protocols of a Common Law Court are summarized in the following outline, which must be followed by anyone seeking to accuse and try other parties.

Step One: Compiling the Case

A Statement of Claim must be produced by those bringing a case, known as the Plaintiffs. Their Statement sets out in point form the basic facts of the dispute, the wrong being alleged, and the relief or remedy being sought.

Next, the Plaintiff's Statement of Claim must be accompanied by supporting evidence: documents and testimonies proving their case beyond any reasonable doubt. This evidence must be duly sworn by those not party to the dispute in the form of witnessed statements; and it must consist of the original documents themselves, and not copies.

As well, anyone whose testimony is used in this body of evidence must be willing to come into Court to testify and affirm their own statement.

Step Two: Seeking the Remedy of a Common Law Court; Filing a Notice of Claim of Right

After gathering his case, a Plaintiff must then seek the aid of a Common Law Court and its officers. Such a Court can be brought into being by publishing a Notice of Claim of Right (*see Court Documents Appendix 4*), which is a public declaration calling for the assistance of the community in the asserting of the Plaintiff's right under Natural Justice to have his case heard through the Common Law, by way of a jury of his neighbors and peers. Such a Notice can be published in local newspapers or simply notarized and posted in a prominent public location, like a town hall or library.

Step Three: Forming a Common Law Court

Within 24 hours of the issuing of such a Notice of Claim of Right, any twelve citizens of a community can constitute themselves as a Common Law Court and its jury, and must then appoint the following Court Officers:

- a *Court Adjudicator,* to advise and oversee the Court

- *a Public or Citizen Prosecutor* to conduct the case; this person is normally the Plaintiff himself or someone he authorizes to advise but not represent him

- *a Defense Counsel* to advise but not represent the accused

- *a Court Sheriff*, either elected from the community or delegated from among existing peace officers

- *Bailiffs, a Court Registrar and a Court Reporter*

It is assumed that people with knowledge of the Common Law and legal procedure will act in these capacities. And, as mentioned, a Common Law Magistrate or Justice of the Peace may also initiate this formation of a Common Law Court.

Step Four: Swearing in and Convening the Jury and Court Officers; Oaths of Office

Upon the appointment of these Court Officers, the Adjudicator (a Justice of the Peace or a comparable Magistrate) will formally convene the Court by taking and administering the following Oath of Common Law Court Office to all of the Court officers:

I (name) will faithfully perform my duties as an officer of this Common Law Court according to the principles of Natural Justice and Due Process, acting at all times with integrity, honesty and lawfulness. I recognize that if I fail to consistently abide by this Oath I can be removed from my Office. I make this public Oath freely, without coercion or ulterior motive, and without mental reservation.

After taking this oath, the Jury members, Court Counselors, Sheriffs, Bailiffs and Reporter will then convene and receive instructions from the Adjudicator concerning the case. The Adjudicator is not a presiding Judge or Magistrate but an advisor to the Court, and has no power to influence, direct or halt the actions or the decisions of the Jury or other Court officers, except in the case of a gross miscarriage of justice or negligence on the part of Court officers. Thus, the Court is self-regulating and dependent on the mutual respect and governance of the Court officers and the Jury.

Step Five: Pretrial Conference

The Adjudicator brings together both parties in a pre-trial conference to settle the case prior to a trial. If a settlement is not achieved, both parties must engage in a mandatory Examination for Discovery where the evidence and statements of both sides will be presented. After a period of not more than one week, this pre-trial conference will conclude and the trial will commence.

Step Six: Issuing a Public Summons

No person or agency may be lawfully summoned into Common Law Court without first receiving a complete set of charges being brought against them and a formal *Notice to Appear, or Writ of Public Summons*. Such a Summons outlines the exact time, date and address when and where the trial will commence.

The Public Summons is applied for by the Plaintiff through the Court Registrar. The Summons will be issued under the signature of the Court Adjudicator and delivered to the Defendant by the Court Sheriff within 24 hours of its filing in the Court Registry by the Plaintiff.

The Sheriff must personally serve the Defendant, or post the Summons in a public place and record the posting if the Defendant avoids service. The Defendant has seven days to appear in Court from the date of service.

Step Seven: The Trial Commences; Opening Arguments

After an introduction by the Adjudicator, the trial commences with opening arguments by first the Plaintiff or Prosecutor, and then the Defendant. The Adjudicator and both Counselors will then have the chance to question either parties for clarification, and to make motions to the Court if it is apparent that the proceedings can be expedited.

Note: Step Seven can still occur even if one side, usually the Defendant, is not present in Court and refuses to participate. Such a trial, being conducted *in absentia*, remains a legitimate legal procedure once the Defendant is given every opportunity to appear and respond to the charges and evidence against him. An *in absentia* trial will commence with the Plaintiff presenting his opening argument followed by his central case. The Court-appointed Defense Counsel will then be given the chance to argue on behalf of the absent Defendant, if that is the wish of the latter.

It is often the case that a non-response or non-appearance by the Defendant can result in the Adjudicator advising the Jury to declare a verdict in favor of the Plaintiff, on the grounds that the Defendant has tacitly agreed with the case against himself by not disputing the evidence or charges, and by making no attempt to appear and defend his own good name in public.

Step Eight: The Main Proceedings

Assuming the proceedings are not being conducted in absentia and the Defendant is present, the main proceedings of the trial then commence with the Plaintiff's presentation of the details of his evidence and argument against the Defendant, who can then respond. The Plaintiff may be assisted by the Citizen Prosecutor.

After his presentation, the Plaintiff is then cross-examined by the Defendant or his advising Counsel. Following cross-examination, the Defendant presents his case, with or without his advising Counselor, and in turn is cross-examined by the Plaintiff or the Citizen

Prosecutor. There are usually no restrictions placed on the duration of the main proceedings.

Step Nine: Closing Arguments and Summaries to the Jury and Final Advice to the Adjudicator

After the main proceedings, the Adjudicator has the chance to further question both parties in order to give final advice to the Jury. The Plaintiff and the Defendant then have the right to give their summary argument to the Court. The Adjudicator closes with any final comments to the Jury.

Step Ten: The Jury Retires to Deliberate

The Court is held in recess while the twelve citizen jury members retire to come to a unanimous verdict and a sentence, based on their appraisal of all the evidence. There is no time restriction on their deliberations, and during that time, they are not allowed contact with anyone save the Court Bailiff, who is their guard. The Jury's verdict and sentence must be consensual and unanimous.

Step Eleven: The Jury Issues its Unanimous Verdict and Sentence

The Court is reconvened after the Jury has come to a verdict. If the jurors are not in complete unanimity concerning the verdict, the defendant is automatically declared to be innocent. The Jury spokesman, chosen from among them by a vote, announces the verdict to the Court, and based on that verdict, the final sentence is also declared by the Jury, or jointly with the Adjudicator.

Step Twelve: The Court Adjourns and the Sentence is Enforced

Following the announcement of the Verdict and Sentence, the Adjudicator either frees the Defendant or affirms and authorizes the decision of the Jury in the name of the Court, and instructs the Sheriff to enforce that sentence. The Adjudicator dismisses the Jury and concludes the trial proceedings. The complete record of the proceedings is a public document, accessible to anyone, and it can in no way be withheld, altered or compromised by the Adjudicator or any other party.

A Note on Common Law Enforcement:

It is understood that every able bodied citizen is obligated and empowered by Natural Law to assist the Court Sheriff and his Deputies in enforcing the sentence of the Court, including by ensuring the imprisonment of the guilty, the monitoring of his associates and the public seizure of the assets and property of the guilty and his agents, if such is the sentence of the Court.

This collective law enforcement is required in the interest of public safety, especially when the guilty party is an entire institution or head officers of that body.

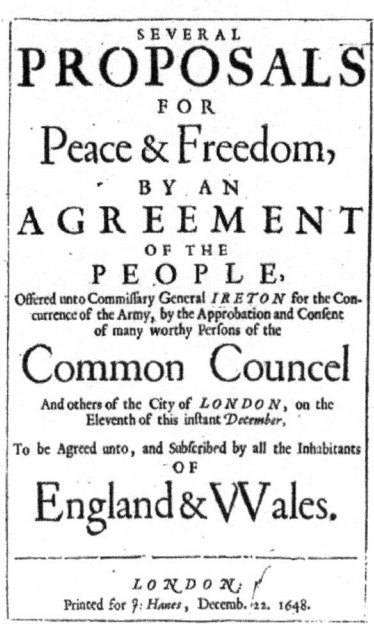

A Note on Appealing Common Law Court Decisions:

Under the doctrine of Natural Law, in which every man and woman is born with an inherent grasp of right and wrong and of justice, it is understood that a jury of twelve citizens, when given the complete evidence and facts of a case, will arrive at a just and proper verdict. The truth of that verdict must stand and is not subject to re-evaluation or dispute, except in the case of a gross dereliction of duty or non-consideration of evidence. Therefore, the verdicts of Common Law Court juries are not subject to appeal or revision, since the truth is not mutable or reformable.

This solidity of a verdict is also required by the Common Law doctrine and custom of *Stare Decisis,* meaning "the decision stands", whereby the precedent decisions of previous Court verdicts have binding authority. Without *Stare Decisis*, the law is subject to the whims and interference of others.

In the words of Black's Law Dictionary,

The doctrine of stare decisis states that legal decisions are binding and shall not be reversed. 'The decision stands.' That is, once a court has entered its judgment upon an issue, it shall not reverse itself. This is in fact the foundation of legality in the Common Law System and is one of the principal differences between Common and Civil Law.

Convictions and Verdicts

Every legal system operates according to its own worldview and essential purpose. In the case of Civil or statute law, the contending interests of individuals waging war with one another in a courtroom define the process and aims of the Court. This system serves whoever has the money or influence to present the most convincing case, usually before a single magistrate who is part of a self-governing and unaccountable judicial clique.

The law, under this elite-derived system, is a private weapon to wield against another person or group over commercial interests, not an avenue of justice for all or of the common good. In the Common Law, contrarily, the Court is defined not by contending individual interests, but by the needs of the community as a whole, and by justice as defined by those who have suffered from the lack of it. A bedrock of collective morality shapes how the Common Law operates, according to a simple issue:

Will this legal decision and precedent best serve the community as a whole, and those within it who are the most vulnerable or who have suffered or been victimized, or who may be?

Men and women have a natural tendency to resolve their differences and mediate disputes among themselves when not coerced and left to themselves to apply their own sense of right and wrong. Despite this, the State has under threat of force violently conditioned people to automatically deny their own judgment and defer to external authorities whenever they are in dispute or they seek justice. And so a long "relearning of freedom" is needed for Common Law to become a functional part of human life once again.

Fortunately, we have found that the very act of publicly declaring and establishing the supremacy of the People and their Common Law has sparked that process of relearning freedom among growing numbers of people. Sparked, but not secured. For the greatest impediment to the efficacy of Common Law courts lies in the fears and doubts that seize citizens when they are presented with the power to be the law, and not have the law be done to them.

We have been taught that taking the law into your own hands is a violation of civil order and tantamount to anarchy. In reality, for citizens to judge legal matters for themselves is the highest civic virtue and the cornerstone of true democracy, according to the Athenian lawmaker Solon. The latter even believed that citizens should be fined or reprimanded for shrinking from a public controversy or from their responsibility to be lawgivers.

At the heart of that personal responsibility for the law is the capacity of citizens to judge a lawsuit for themselves as sworn jurors, and impose a verdict and sentence in such a suit. The jury system has always been the purest expression of the Common Law and its capacity to empower the people themselves to defend traditional liberties and ascertain the truth of a matter.

To render a fair and reasonable verdict, anyone simply needs to know all the facts and the evidence, and consider it all soberly, without threats, influence or coercion.

The more people who gather to determine the truth of a matter, the more likely they will come to a just and truthful verdict. It tends to be the case that individual bias or prejudice, which is always present and undeniable within a jury, becomes through the jury process counterbalanced and absorbed into a broader collective truth imposed by the natural reason and fairness among jury members.

Enforcement

The big and thorny issue, of course, is not whether men and women can come to a Court verdict, but rather, how their decision can be enforced, and effective in their community. This is especially an issue when the verdict is imposed against heads of church or state, or even entire institutions, as in the February 25, 2013 verdict of the International Common Law Court of Justice (ICLCJ) concerning Genocide in Canada. (_www.itccs.org_, _www.murderbydecree.com_)

To use that case as an example, the moral weight of the verdict was clearly the strongest weapon in the arsenal of the Court, and created the conditions for the enforcement of the verdict against the thirty officials of church and state named in the indictment.

For one thing, the February 25 verdict – which sentenced all the defendants to public banishment, twenty five years in prison and the loss of property and assets – directly helped depose not only Pope Benedict, Joseph Ratzinger, but the most powerful Catholic Cardinal in Rome: the Vatican Secretary of State Tarcisio Bertone, who also resigned while in office after the ICLCJ verdict was pronounced.

Ratzinger and Bertone know about international law, even if others don't. They clearly understood that the verdict of the ICLCJ carries a recognized legitimacy under the Law of Nations and the public right to form Tribunals of Conscience when governments and courts refuse to address a matter. And the Vatican also knows that the ICLCJ verdict can be entered into other nation's courts and used for the issuing of arrest warrants against proven war criminals like church officers.

And so the resignation of these ostensibly "untouchable" church leaders in the spring of 2013 is simple proof of the power of independent, common law court verdicts. A court verdict, after all, is a binding order carrying with it the full force of the law, and whoever ignores or subverts such a verdict, and the Court's orders arising from it, is guilty of an indictable crime.

In our website ***www.itccs.org*** we have reprinted all of the Court documents from that first ICLCJ case of Genocide in Canada. The Court Order and Arrest Warrant dated March 5, 2013, can be acted on by any sworn agent of the ICLCJ or whoever such an Agent appoints. Any citizen, in short, can assist in the arrest of Joseph Ratzinger, Tarcisio Bertone and the other officials of church and state found guilty of Crimes against Humanity by the ICLCJ.

Such enforcement of the law by citizens themselves is generally recognized in most countries, under the precedent known generically as a right of Citizens Arrest. In Canada, for example, under a law known as the Citizens Arrest and Self-Defence Act (2012), citizens can detain anyone who either commits a crime or is even suspected of having done so, or who poses a threat to their own or others' safety; like, for our purposes, a child raping priest. This power of citizens' arrest has been broadened under this new Canadian law, from what it was previously.
(*see:* *http://laws-lois.justice.gc.ca/eng/annualstatutes/2012_9/FullText.html*)

In theory, then, the enforcement of Common Law Court verdicts by any citizen is not only legitimate and lawful, but is guaranteed even under the laws of countries dominated by Civil, statute law. But power, as we know, is not only about laws and theory, but ultimately involves naked force: the capacity of one group to impose its will upon another.

Hugh Grotius, a sixteenth century pioneer of international law, said that legal principles acquired power only when backed by cannon fire. So besides its legal and moral weight, what "cannons" will back up and enforce the verdicts of our Common Law courts? Especially when the fire power of those we are arresting and sentencing is apparently so much greater than ours?

Another great pioneer, the Chinese general Sun Tzu, wrote millennia ago that in any conflict, power is not ultimately what you have materially but rather psychologically; and the superior firepower of a much bigger enemy can always be negated with the right, unforeseen maneuvers. (*We reprinted some of Sun Tzu most relevant teachings below*) [See Appendix 6]

Those rulers indicted by the ICLCJ are people garbed by the illusory robes of their offices, and they are guarded by other men and women who, like the rulers themselves, are motivated primarily by fear. That fear is their greatest weakness, and can be easily exploited by even a small group of people, as anyone who has occupied a Roman Catholic Church learns very quickly.

The fact that laws guard the rich and the powerful is not as important as the reality that any functional law rests upon its moral and political legitimacy. Once such legitimacy is weakened or gone, the laws and hard physical power of a state or church begin to crumble. Once public confidence in a ruler wanes, internal divisions appear in the ruling hierarchy, and usually a "palace coup" occurs and the regime falls.

We are witnessing precisely such developments and such a collapse of legitimacy within the Roman Catholic Church today, in the manner of events prior to the deposing of any dictatorship. And so the short answer to the question, how do we enforce our verdicts in the face of the power of the enemy, is simply, we do as Sun Tzu teaches, and strike at the weakest, not the strongest, part of that enemy.

The weak point of any institution, especially a church, is its public image and its source of money. Threaten either, and the entire institution must respond to the smallest of enemies. We have proven that in practice. And the very fact of our smallness gives us a freedom and flexibility to strike at such big targets when and how we like: a power that is denied to big institutions.

A Common Law Court verdict like the one of February 25, 2013, is a wedge between the credibility of an institution like the Vatican and the rest of the world. By striking at that credibility – a weak link in the church's chain – we are maneuvering around the strong points of that opponent and hitting them where they have no defense: the fact that as an organization, they officially protect and aid child rapists and human trafficking. And it was precisely through such a strategic maneuver that on August 4, 2013, the Vatican was declared a Transnational Criminal body under international law.

As such a criminal body, the Vatican can now be legally disestablished, its officers arrested, and its property and wealth seized, not simply under Common Law but according to the Law of Nations. (*see The United Nations Convention against Transnational Organized Crime, November 2000, articles 5, 6 and 12:* http://www.unodc.org/unodc/treaties/CTOC/#Fulltext)

So while it isn't normally possible to immediately detain heads of states or corporations after a sentence is passed against them, such an arrest does follow naturally as their credibility and protection diminishes. Their overt power tends to crumble as the law and public condemnation works around their strong defenses and undermines them, like water flowing around a wall or a rock.

The point of any Common Law Court verdict, after all, is not to target or imprison mere individuals, but to stop any threat to the helpless and to the community: to arrest such threats so they do not reoccur, primarily by ending the institutional source of those threats. And our chief means to do so is the moral weight of our evidence and verdicts combined with the capacity of many people to enforce those verdicts.

Common Law Sheriffs and Peace Officers

That brings us to a key aspect of the Court: its police arm, without which it cannot function.

The tradition of Common Law sheriffs is an old one in the English speaking world: men or women appointed from the local community to detain those harming others, bring them into town or "shire" courts for judgment, and enforce that court's sentence. In the United States, that tradition is still alive and embodied in locally elected sheriffs who are granted considerable power within their communities.

The role of the Common Law Court Sheriff is fourfold: to provide security for the Court, to deliver Court Summonses and Orders to Appear, to detain and physically deliver to Court those summoned who evade a Court Order, and to enforce the final sentence of the Court, including by jailing and monitoring the guilty.

The Sheriff does not perform these duties alone, but with deputies and other agents he appoints to assist him. Such a "posse" is another pejorative term that actually refers to an important traditional custom of mobilizing all the able bodied men in a community to stop anyone who has committed a crime. The word "posse" comes from a Latin term *pro (toto) posse suo* meaning "to do the utmost in one's power".

According to one writer,

"All persons who were the victims of a crime in Anglo-Saxon England were expected to raise their 'hue and cry' and apprehend the criminal; and upon hearing their cry, every able-bodied man in the community was expected to do the 'utmost in his power' [pro toto posse suo] to chase and apprehend to accused as a "posse." **1215: The Year of Magna Carta** by J. Danziger et al (2003)

The custom of electing community peace officers like sheriffs, in other words, arose from the belief that everyone in a community had the obligation to police and protect themselves and their children. The Court Sheriff is thereby the servant of the people, taken from among them, answerable to and recallable by them, and not an external force over them.

Part of the power of such a Sheriff is that he can deputize anyone to assist him, *including other police officers and agents of the very institutions being named and tried in Common Law courts.* **This is an especially important tactic and action during this, the early stages of the development of our local Common Law courts, since it uses the very strength of the system we are opposing against itself.**

To give an example, if a Common Law Court Summons or Arrest Warrant is to be delivered against a church or government official, the Court Sheriff will first deliver a copy of it to the local, existing police agency along with a Deputizing Notice placing those police under the jurisdiction of the Common Law. *(See Court Documents in Appendix 4)* As such, the police are then obligated to assist the Sheriff and must take the same Oath of Common Law Office as the Sheriff.

If those issued such a Notice deny or dispute it or refuse to take the Oath, they are then ordered to stand down from their position and to not interfere with the Sheriff in his duties. If they agree with the Notice, either directly or through their silence or non-interference, such police agencies are tacitly abiding by the Common Law action, and the normal protection around criminals in high office is suddenly nullified. We should not underestimate the revolutionary consequences of such a nullifications: mainly, that the shield around the powerful is suddenly gone.

Such a remarkable encounter is in effect an enormous tug of war between two contending legal systems: a battle of wills, played out in full public view as an enormous teaching moment. *Our aim is to create and encourage such a creative confrontation and moral conflict at every level of official society.*

This is the bigger and crucial point of such a confrontation between Court Sheriffs and Civil law policemen: a clash that must always be visible and televised to the world as it occurs. For this brings with it a chance for the people to learn directly that those policemen and soldiers who provide the muscle for the system are not exempt from the authority of Common Law *and must ultimately make a choice concerning who and what they serve.* The moral and social impact of publicly posing such a question is inestimable.

We were there every day, trying to talk to the young soldiers about the killers they were defending.

Nothing we said seemed to get through to them until the day we began reading out the names of the people who were tortured to death.

Then I saw one young National Guardsman start to wink back his tears.

And I knew we would win.

Barbara Stelling, 1969

On those occasions when this tactic has been tested in Canada and elsewhere, the results have always been the same: the police back off and do not interfere. Time and again, neither the RCMP nor the Vancouver police have interfered with protestors who peacefully occupied the churches responsible for the death of Indian children. On one occasion, a senior police sergeant even stated that if the Catholic church had committed such crimes and were served with a Court Order, he would be duty bound to enforce such an Order and arrest those responsible!

Again, quoting Sun Tzu, to defeat an enemy one must know them; and such knowledge can only be gained through constant contact. As he says,

"Provoke them to learn their responses. Prick them to test their strength and weakness. Do not outfight them but out think them."

Common Law peace officers return power to the people by making them their own police authorities. In so doing, they challenge the very basis of the status-quo and its elite-based rule, by undermining those unaccountable "armed bodies of men" who constitute the final and ultimate power of the State. The Common Law, in short, is a seed of fundamental social and political transformation, not simply a weapon of self-defense for the oppressed.

On Citizens' Arrest

The right and necessity of citizens to detain suspected or actual criminals has long been recognized under both civil and common law. For example, as mentioned, under a recent law in Canada, The Citizens' Arrest and Self Defense Act (2012), the right of citizens to perform arrests and detain suspects on their own has been broadened to include not only people caught endangering the community or harming others, but anyone suspected of crimes, including known offenders.

Under the same common law custom of pro toto posse suo (see above) that empowers any group of adults to unite and stop those causing harm, the right of Citizens' Arrest is not restricted or negated by a higher authority because of the recognition that any man or woman has the competence and obligation to see and directly halt wrongdoing in their community.

The procedure for performing a Citizens' Arrest is as follows:

1. One must first either witness a crime, or recognize a suspected criminal or known offender, or even have a reasonable suspicion that such persons pose a danger to others. Such a suspicion must be based on probable cause and not simply a "feeling" or prejudice about someone.

2. One must then inform the suspect or offender that he or she is being placed under Citizens' Arrest under the right of Necessity to Defend, which obligates the arrester to detain the suspect or offender. The arresting party must state who they are and why they are exercising the power of arrest by stating the cause of action.

3. The offender or suspect must then be detained and held for trial in a common law court, if they turn out to have committed a crime or pose a danger to others. The amount of force used in the arrest must be a reasonable response to the

suspect's behavior.

Citizens can normally hand over those they have detained to an authorized Common Law peace officer or a Sheriff of the court. The arresting parties must be willing to appear in court and give sworn testimony concerning their actions.

The crucial importance of the power of Citizens' Arrest is that it trains and empowers citizens to take responsibility for policing their communities and for the law itself. It moves democracy from theory to action.

Broader Consequences of the Common Law Court: A World made New

Our first real step towards independence from England was the establishment of our own Republican courts, right under the nose of the Brits. We set up a different legal system of our traditional Brehon laws, even while under military occupation. And we had to defend that system in arms. So you can say that once we started living under our own laws, everything else had to follow, right up to becoming a new nation.

 - Joe MacInnes, Republican veteran of the Irish Civil War (1974 interview)

For what you call the Law is but a club of the rich over the lowest of men, sanctifying the conquest of the earth by a few and making their theft the way of things. But over and above these pitiful statutes of yours that enclose the common land and reduce us to poverty to make you fat stands the Law of Creation, which renders judgment on rich and poor alike, making them one. For freedom is the man who will thus turn the world upside down, therefore no wonder he has enemies. - Gerard Winstanlley, The true Leveller Standard, Surrey England 1649

For the people themselves to sit in judgment of historically untouchable rulers like popes and heads of state, and to render an enforceable verdict on their crimes, is a revolutionary act. And such a revolution has begun, with the February 25, 2013 verdict of the International Common Law Court of Justice.

 We cannot shrink from or deny the profound consequences of taking such a necessary historic step. Rather, we must recognize that the new judicial system in our hands is in fact a doorway to a transformed world, in which the land and its wealth and society as a whole is reclaimed by all people, and brought into harmony with Natural Justice through a great social leveling.

Many traditions and prophecies foresee such a time as now as a judgment upon the corruption and injustice of the human world. Biblically, such a moment was known as the Jubilee, when all human laws and divisions are abolished, and society, like nature during a fallow year, is allowed to rest from warfare, corruption and injustice.

In truth, we recognize this historic moment not only as a condemnation of what has been, but as a transformation into what is coming to be: a reinventing of humanity according to the simple principle that no law or authority shall ever again cause anyone to rule, harm or dominate others.

The aim of Common Law is to re-establish direct relations of mutual aid among people by placing justice and the law within their reach again. And that devolution of power will simultaneously disestablish all hierarchical institutions of state, business and church which control and mediate human life as a power over people.

A process so profound and revolutionary can only be enacted from the grassroots, by many people who have relearned freedom and use it to take action in their own communities to govern themselves as their own judge, jury and police. On the basis of this good renewed soil, a great harvest will one day arise in the form of new and local Republics of Equals, in harmony with humanity and all Creation. The Common Law is a catalyst and a means towards achieving this political and spiritual end.

For now, as we struggle to give birth to the Courts that are like a great plow breaking open the dead soil of the status-quo, we must never forget that much of what we have been taught will betray us, for we have been raised as slaves to think and operate under laws that serve the few. Everything must be rethought and retried according to the three great Principles of Natural Law:

All things are placed in common for the good of all; no-one has any natural authority over another; and therefore, the law shall cause harm to no-one.

Our principles are firm, but our methods and tactics are supple. We must audaciously try ever-new ways to expose, indict and stop the criminal institutions and corporations that are killing our planet, our children and our sacred liberties. And together, we must learn from every mistake and defeat, and generalize the victories and wisdom we gain into clear precedent, throughout this long redemptive struggle that will span many lifetimes.

The conscience born into us is our lamp during this journey and our best instructor, as is our great heritage of Natural Law and Reason, passed down to us so that a free and independent humanity may never perish from the earth.

Armed with this truth, this knowledge and this sacred purpose, go forth and take action! You have a world to win back.

The Law is the public conscience. And the Common Law is but common reason. - Sir Edward Coke, 1622

"It does not take a majority to prevail... but rather an irate, tireless minority, keen on setting brushfires of freedom in the minds of men."

Samuel Adams

Appendix 1: The Sovereign Basis of Common Law Courts

The Commons of England assembled in Parliament declare that the people under God are the origin of all just power and have the supreme authority of the nation. Whatsoever is enacted and declared law by the Commons alone has the force of law, and all the people are included thereby, with or without the consent of the king. - An Act to Establish the High Court of Justice, House of Commons, London, January 4, 1649

Where does your authority come from? That challenge confronts anyone standing under the common law and its courts. But in truth, no such court can lawfully operate without a legitimating power behind it: namely, a constitutional Assembly of the people that authorizes common law courts. Those assemblies may be local or national, but they must establish a sovereign jurisdiction within which the courts can operate.

Such an Assembly in England, known as the Commons or Parliament, created the High Court of Justice that lawfully deposed and executed King Charles I in 1649 as a tyrant and war criminal. For ultimately all legal power derives from a Constitution established by free men and women gathered as equal sovereigns under God and the natural law. If our courts do not have such a sanction they are merely a private weapon in the hands of a few, and thereby they mimic the autocracy of de-facto rulers.

That is, no common law court that we establish can operate without a sovereign Assembly and Constitution behind it. In Canada, England and other "crown lands" that new Constitutional Assembly has to be created; in republics like America they must be reclaimed and re-established. But in any event, the struggle to create common law courts cannot be separated from the wider political campaign to create such sovereign Republics, which alone can sanction and legitimate these courts.

The fact that our effort to create common law courts is beginning locally and among small groups of people is not impeded by this need for an overarching political authority behind the courts. For any number of citizens can and must first gather in local assemblies to covenant themselves into a new power that can establish common law courts. The will to convene together precedes the court and grants it a popular jurisdiction and authority that no power can undo.

In the words of John Cooke, the prosecutor of Charles Stuart in 1649, *The people sit in judgment of all rulers, yea even kings, for only in the people has God granted the authority to make laws and enact them. From such a mandate do we sit today as a High Court and jury, as an expression of the free will of the Commons in Parliament.*

Source: The Tyrannicide Brief by Geoffrey Robertson (2005) and The Basis for the Republic of Kanata and of England: The History and Lawfulness of the Abolition of the "Crown" - A Brief Survey of Constitutional and Legal Precedents (www.itccs.org , 2016)

Appendix 2: **The Peoples' Assemblies: A Vision and A Practical Guide**

The Revolution may have been affected first in the hearts and minds of the People, but it took shape in our Constitutional Conventions, where the People learned how to hold and wield power for themselves. – **John Adams, 1791**

The Commons of England assembled in Parliament declare that the people under God are the origin of all just power, and have the supreme authority of the nation. Whatsoever is enacted and declared law by the Commons alone has the force of law, and all the people are included thereby, with or without the consent of the king. - **An Act to Establish the High Court of Justice, House of Commons, London, January 4, 1649**

Under this Proclamation, all lawful authority now resides in the People gathered in an elected Congress and other governmental bodies established by the People under Common Law. – **A Public Proclamation abolishing Crown Authority in Canada, January 15, 2015**

……………..

Making the Common Law Republic a Working Reality

We begin by recognizing that the old regimes and their de facto law are part of a criminal corporatocracy that is hopelessly corrupt and self-serving, and is an oppressive weight on we, the people. It has lost its right to govern.

Growing numbers of people are re-learning their inborn freedom and reclaiming the law and the land for themselves. Great movements of liberation are like a mighty rush of steam, rising from below to topple tyranny and remake the world. And yet without the right piston, that steam is dissipated and lost.

The dream of a sovereign Republic of Equals known dwells for now in thousands of men and women, but it still lacks a great piston to harness and unite these people, and join them with the rest of the country. Such a mechanism to build a new nation from the ground up is the Peoples' Assemblies.

The Assemblies are lawful bodies that are actively replacing the old regime. They arise from the Natural Law understanding that the People, or The Commons, gathered in elected and self-governing congregations, are the source of all legal, political and spiritual authority; and that whatever they enact is sovereign and binding, and not subject to any other power.

The Peoples' Assemblies are the means by which we can build a new society in the shell of the old. They are citizen-run legislative bodies based in local communities that will increasingly replace existing governments: in effect, a functioning "dual power".

In the Assemblies, laws are regularly introduced, debated and enacted by the people directly. These Assemblies are in effect schools of revolution and direct democracy, where the people can learn how to make the law and govern themselves in their own name.

By their nature as a replacement of the existing local authorities, the Assemblies are a direct challenge to the legal and political power of the existing governments. Accordingly, from the outset the Assemblies must be protected by the people themselves, organized in a Militia. And since their purpose is to unite people under a new jurisdiction and pass legislation, the Assemblies will give birth as well to common law courts in their communities.

These three aspects – the Assembly, its Militia, and its Courts – are the basic local features of a new common law Republic. All of these three arms of the Republic will work together to reclaim the entire country for all of the people, and develop new rurally based egalitarian communities to embody our sovereignty. In a practical sense, the Assemblies will provide our new young movement with a much bigger "pond" in which to swim and grow, since they will draw into Republican debate and action many more people.

For example, one of the first tasks of the Peoples' Assemblies, and a popular drawing card for many citizens, will be to reclaim all tax monies and payments presently being sent to Ottawa, the provinces and other "crown" authorities. Local Republican banks or credit unions will be established by the Assemblies as a repository of this reclaimed wealth of the people: funds that will be used to build up our communities according to the will of the people.

In short, the Assemblies will be a practical means to directly reclaim the wealth and the land of the world for all of the people under the authority of the Republic, including by seizing and sharing out the land, bank accounts and properties of the old regime.

Finally, the Assemblies are the skeletal framework for the entire Republic by serving as the means for electing delegates to the national Congress and regional bodies.

Practical Measures

A Peoples' Assembly is established by any group of twelve or more people who covenant to gather regularly according to a Charter issued by the Republic. This body is then self-governing but linked to the Republic through its Executive and delegates.

The Assembly is open without restriction to all men and women in the local community, to debate any issue and introduce, debate and pass any law. All participants must recognize the authority of the Assembly and abide by to its procedures and aims.

The Assembly is chaired by an elected Convener and administered by a Corresponding Secretary, who is a liaison with other Assemblies. A common law Sheriff provides security for the Assembly, and is responsible for raising and training a local Citizens' Militia.

The Assembly will also establish common law courts to enforce and adjudicate the laws that it passes.

The Assemblies must meet on a regular basis in the same visible, public place: one that is conducive to large numbers of people. It is recommended that once established, the Peoples' Assembly will convene on the first Monday of every month as an entire body, and every week in its Executive capacity. The sessions of the Assembly can last as long as is deemed necessary.

A Constitution will govern the operation of the Peoples' Assembly and the actions of its officers and Executive. The latter will have the authority to discipline or expel Assembly participants according to this Constitution, and to instruct the Assembly's Sheriff and Militia to enforce its lawful rulings and any other measures necessary to protect the Assembly.

The Assembly is established as the only lawful, representative body of direct democracy in local communities. As such, it is the alternative local government for all people to join and thereby leave their former "crown" or corporate allegiances, including the police, judges and civil servants.

Accordingly, every effort must be made by the Assembly to win over and deputize the agents of the former regimes and incorporate them into our new Republican institutions of Peoples' Assembly, Citizens' Militia, and Common Law Courts. Yet we must also vigilantly screen these former officials to ensure their commitment and loyalty to our new Republic.

A Charter to Establish and Maintain a Sovereign Peoples' Assembly under the authority of the Republic of Kanata

LET IT BE KNOWN AND ACKNOWLEDGED that under the Natural Law, it is the Unalienable Right of the People as sovereign men and women to covenant into self-governing bodies to enact laws and provide for the safety and liberty of their families and communities;

Therefore, We, the Undersigned, do hereby establish such a freely elected Peoples' Assembly as a self-regulating and elected legislative and legal body, subject to no other authority except other such free Assemblies whose delegates are gathered in a Republican Congress;

We, the Undersigned, do solemnly swear to maintain and defend to the death this sovereign Peoples' Assembly as a just, lawful body that is the voice and the safeguard of the people of our community;

We swear to govern ourselves and this Assembly according to its Constitution and the Common Law, relying on the people and their Militia and on their common law courts for its safety and wellbeing.

We, the Undersigned, do hereby set our Oath and names to this Charter, here, in the

Community of _____ on this _____ Day of _____ In the Year _____

Constitution of the Sovereign Peoples' Assembly

Article One - Name

The Assembly shall be designated as The Sovereign Peoples' Assembly of (name of community).

Article Two - Purpose

The Assembly shall be an elected self-governing body of the People established to introduce, debate and enact any laws or regulations decided by the People, and to generally govern and protect the community under the rule of the Common Law and the authority and Constitution of the Republic of Kanata.

Article Three – Authority and Power

The Assembly is a de jure sovereign body not subject to any other authority besides that of similar sovereign Assemblies whose delegates gather in an elected Republican Congress. It shall have the full and undivided power of a governing legislative body, unrestricted by veto or interference, including the power to levy taxes, raise a Citizens' Militia, seize and reclaim the wealth, land and properties of the nation, and establish and maintain local Common Law courts of justice.

Article Four - Convention

The Assembly shall be convened in an accessible public place on the first Monday of every month at 10 am. It shall remain in session according to the will of its participants.

Article Five – Structure

The Assembly shall act as a body at large in all of its deliberations, according to a majority vote system of either open or closed balloting, and according to this Constitution. The Assembly shall be administered by an elected Convener, who shall preside at and chair all sessions of the Assembly, and by an Executive body and

Corresponding Secretary. The Executive shall meet separately every week to maintain the daily operations of the Assembly, its courts and its Militia.

Article Six – Establishment

The Assembly shall be established by the common agreement and pledge of at least twelve men or women in a community, under a Charter issued under the authority of the Republic of Kanata. The original signatories to this Charter shall assume no guaranteed role or privilege within the Assembly unless thus delegated and elected to a position by the People in Assembly.

Article Seven – Adjunct bodies

Either the Assembly as a whole or the Executive body shall have the power to create the following officers and bodies under the authority of the Assembly and this Constitution:

1. A Citizens' Militia to safeguard the safety and liberty of the Assembly and the community as a whole
2. A Sheriff and staff of deputies to provide security to the Assembly and to raise and train the Citizens' Militia
3. Local common law courts
4. Official delegates to represent the Assembly and the local community within a wider Republican Congress
5. Local Republican banks or credit unions to safeguard the wealth of the community
6. Land trusts and cooperative rural communities
7. Special Commissions and Grand Juries of the Assembly to investigate and make recommendations.
8. Any other body required for the wellbeing of the Assembly and the People

Article Eight – Limitations

Neither the Assembly nor its Executive nor any adjunct body shall enact any legislation, regulation or course of action that is contrary either to this Constitution or to the Constitution of the Republic of Kanata and its common law. The Executive of the Assembly shall have no veto or nullification power over the decisions of the Assembly unless those decisions violate the terms of this Constitution.

Article Nine – Term of Office

The Convener of the Assembly shall have a term of office of one year, and may not serve more than three consecutive terms. The Corresponding Secretary and other Executive positions shall operate for terms of office established by the Assembly. All Assembly Sheriffs shall be elected for a term of office of one year.

Article Ten – Amendments

This Constitution may be amended by vote of three quarters (75%) of the members of the Assembly, provided these amendments do not violate the Constitution and common law of the Republic of Kanata.

Appendix 3: The Purpose and Nature of our Struggle

By Kevin D. Annett

Whoever grasps and holds onto the essential energy (shih) of a situation will control the outcome of any battle and the fate of any opponent, no matter how powerful they are. – Sun Tzu, The Art of War

Men always begin revolutions with their eyes fixed on the past. – Frederich Engels

What is nothing has been chosen to bring to nothing all the things that are. – 1 Corinthians 1:28

…………………..

Imagine for a moment the present global tyranny not simply as a visible system of corporatism, violence and corruption, but as a vast energy transfer, sucking the vitality and life from billions of people and the biosphere itself into one massive machine. Call that machine whatever you like; its nature and behavior is geared towards a single purpose, and that is the absorption of life into itself. It is one enormous feeder, and we are its morsels.

To first understand this simple truth equips us inwardly to stop this insatiable complex and our participation in it, far better than can mere political analysis. But understanding alone does not free us to act.

All interactions in our universe involve an essential energy that guides the movement of every particle, and determines every outcome. Sun Tzu called this energy "*shih*"; Plato saw it as a pre-existing essence behind the mask of appearances. Some like to call it God. Regardless of its nomenclature, this Source that binds our reality is like a mighty river which can either sweep us along helplessly, or be utilized by us to alter reality. Every ruler understands this simple fact, even while the rest of us have been trained not to grasp it, and thereby are kept eyeless in a harness held by a few.

Those who understand and utilize this "*shih*" are able to control the thoughts and actions of the multitudes of humanity only as long as the latter are devoid of their own access to *shih*. The primary means of stripping humanity of attaining its normally inherent *shih*-power is by using fear and trauma based conditioning at a very young age to cause people to habitually surrender and defer at every level to some "higher" external power, and thereby transfer their own particle of *shih* to that power.

Such an unending energy transfer from the many to the few is the basis of all elite rule in our world. And yet such a system is inherently unstable, since following Natural Law, the nature of *shih* as with any energy system is to disseminate equally and be held in common, and not privately: a fact that invalidates as contrary to the natural order all individual rule, whether by kings, presidents, popes or corporate oligarchies.

We know from our own experience that the loss of *shih* from the many to the few is not simply unnatural and disharmonious; it is so constant and systemic that it cannot be resisted by individual effort alone, since our individuality has been conditioned to operate habitually rather than consciously. We think like we eat – automatically – and therefore without *shih*. For instance, when faced with political repression by the *shih*-holders, our first reflex is to surrender our *shih* once again to them by "pressuring" them to give us justice through ritualized protest and petitioning, relying on their courts and government.

We do not seem capable of shifting our attention away from the *shih*-holders simply because we have no working experience of what our own *shih* actually is. And thus like any lost child, we cannot try to change our world without continually deferring to the "powers that be", whether that be a sympathetic judge, or a "progressive" politician, or even a spiritual adviser. Our imprinted slavery makes it impossible for us to collectively reclaim ourselves, and our world.

Erasing a conditioned imprint may begin within the individual, but it is not manifested individualistically; for collectivity is the nature of universal *shih*, which binds all phenomena in a "mutual garment of destiny and interconnectedness". In any successful revolution, the personal awakening of individuals inexorably causes a collective ripple effect in many other hearts and minds that generates a new kind of "group *shih*": one that is unalterably opposed to the *shih* of the rulers. This new energy system is a living and working counter-culture that draws energy and power away from the rulers and their system, and returns it to the multitude of people, provided they can hold onto it as a group by retaining their own new and separate identity.

The very nature and purpose of our struggle today is to achieve precisely such a new energy dynamic, and allow all of humanity to reclaim their natural *shih* and the collective liberty that it bestows. This purpose must continually guide our thoughts, words and deeds.

Applying Shih Knowledge to our Present Situation

The Chinese general Sun Tzu, writing thousands of years ago, had the best practical understanding of how such an awareness of the essential energy behind reality can and must be used in concrete struggles, especially in war and politics. "Nothing is permanent in life except conflict and change" he wrote in his **Art of War**. "One either masters the *shih* of one's opponent or is mastered by it."

If we set aside our western philosophical bias that dualistically separates matter from spirit, we recognize that Sun Tzu is accurately describing the dance that occurs in any conflict with an adversary. As he writes,

"Enemies, like all opposites, are mutually dependent on one another, being part of a greater unity and purpose. Thus, enemies are defeated not by their abolition but by their absorption into that greater whole."

In short, we can win any engagement not by outnumbering or crushing an opponent, but by re-directing his own essential energy into the outcome we desire.

A classic example of the power of such an approach is found from our own campaign in Canada to indict church and state for Genocide. That campaign, consisting of a few dozen of us in three cities, successfully forced Canada and its churches to respond on our terms by admitting their crime and helping to commence their own dissolution. For by acceding to a new reality, the old matrix called "Christian Canada" surrendered to us its *shih*, and helped energize our agenda of disestablishing Crown and Church: a process that is continuing now to unfold. This new power alignment is crumbling Canada and laying the basis for a new *shih* arrangement that we call the Republic of Kanata.

What achieved this victory were not our numbers but our strategic position, our visible persistence, and our ability to out maneuver and re-direct the *shih* of the system, armed as we were with an undeniable truth and evidence that kept both church and state constantly fearful and on the defensive.

Similarly but even more stunning is the other, greater victory that flowed from this first one: namely, the blow against the Vatican in Rome, and our historic deposing of Pope Benedict in February 2013 by our public conviction of him and other top catholic officials for the same genocide.

This successful mastering by us of a hugely more powerful opponent's *shih* happened because our small movement deliberately used a strategy of guerilla warfare, which is summed up by Sun Tzu thus:

First, when I am few and my enemy is many, I can use the few to strike the many because those whom I battle are restricted, being larger and more unwieldy. Their strength thereby becomes their weakness.

Second, do not respond to the ground your enemy has prepared for you, but instead, shape their ground. Then they have no alternative but to be led by you, as if it was their own idea.

Third, hide the time of battle from an enemy, and make what he loves and defends your first objective. By aiming at and seizing what the enemy holds dear, their greater strength and plans are rendered useless, and they must stop and respond on your terms, no matter how small are your forces.

Thus, on March 17, 2008 during Palm Sunday services, two of our action groups occupied without warning the largest catholic cathedrals in Vancouver and Toronto, making headlines across Canada with our demand that the genocidal churches be prosecuted and forced to return the remains of the Indian children they killed. We also announced that we were commencing an international court action to charge Canada with genocide.

Less than a month later, the government announced for the first time an "inquiry" into the missing residential school children. This led directly to the official Parliamentary "apology" just three months later, in July 2008, and the subsequent official admission by Ottawa that genocide did indeed occur in Canada.

By striking unexpectedly at the Achilles' heel of the main instigator of genocide – behind its own lines, amidst its most "sacred" ritual - we not only shocked and frightened the enemy but created the field of battle and forced our opponent in its fear to respond on our terms. Since then, no-one in Canada has dared anymore to deny that children were killed in the residential schools, and that it was indeed genocide. A few of us thereby reshaped the national narrative; or, in Sun Tzu's words, we mastered the *shih* of an enormous adversary and re-directed it on our terms.

Similarly, the shock wave that deposed Pope Benedict has continued to spread, forcing four other resignations by top Vatican officials named in our common law court indictments, and compelling an enormous and desperate public relations effort by the present "pope" to shore up Rome's collapsing credibility. What is this but living proof of the ability of a small force to absorb the *shih* of the biggest and oldest enemy imaginable: the Vatican Incorporated?

Compare these stunning victories by a handful of people with the negligible results of many thousands of protestors standing outside government buildings and waving placards, and thereby surrendering their collective *shih* to their adversary. For the unstated message of any group of protestors to some external power is clearly this: *We acknowledge your authority; you have the power, not us. All we ask is that you change things for us.* This is not change on the terms of the people, but accommodation to elite rule, regardless of the outcome.

This impotence called protest, like voting or "going through the courts", is in truth the clearest example of the energy-sucking nature of the machine that relies on such controlled "opposition" to feed its own *shih*.

In reality, no such diminishing of peoples' own *shih* is ever required. For the ability for any sized group to capture the *shih* of the government and any corporate regime has been proven in practice. In energetic terms, this constitutes a reclaiming of power in order to rebalance *shih*, whose nature is to disseminate and be shared equally. This approach is the only sure means of changing the nature of power, and thereby bringing down tyranny. And yet as we noted, understanding this truth does not automatically make it happen, for the simple fact that we are a very part of what it is we oppose.

The Symbiotic Nature of Shih

It is often remarked – usually as a justification for not getting involved in a radical movement – that "All revolutions just end replacing one tyrant with another". From a distance, history seems to bear this out.

The moments where masses of people shake off their chains and govern themselves directly and consciously seem to be episodic and brief; most of the time, the "masses" appear to be like a passive herd led around by some elite or another. But this appearance is in fact illusory; people's acquiescence to a regime is not the same thing as them actively supporting it. People will act to change things only when they can see and feel that there exists a working alternative to the status quo: that is, only when they are able to recognize and establish a new collective *shih*. But why does this not seem to happen very often? What is the bulwark that holds people back?

These questions can only be answered in practice by knowing first the symbiotic and interdependent nature of all power and its *shih*. Just as darkness and light depend on one another and are aspects of the same phenomenon, so too are opponents in any war or political change. Even the Biblical "war in heaven" was fought between two types of angels, Lucifer in fact meaning a "being of light". Any struggle is ultimately a dance between the same entity wearing different masks. Just as *shih*, like water, always seeks the lowest and most common ground, so does any conflict: conscious or not, both sides search for a new symbiosis by which both can survive and prosper.

For this reason, it is impossible for any group of citizens to establish a new society within the framework and institutions of the old regime, since all of their thoughts and hopes are conditioned by it. As Frederich Engels observed so accurately following the aborted European insurrections of 1848, "Men always begin revolutions with their eyes fixed on the past." And the Italian rebel Giuseppe Garibaldi, who briefly overturned the papacy in 1870, wrote, "One cannot secure the support of the people by calling for an overthrow of society, but instead by assuring them that their security will be preserved by the changes we envision."

Not surprisingly, such "pragmatic", backward-looking approaches of power-seeking rebels created no new society, and in fact ended up duplicating the regimes they fought. Nineteenth century European radicals had not read Sun Tzu; nor, for that matter, have most of today's erstwhile rebels.

To establish a new collective *shih*, we must not resist or combat the old regime but absorb its own *shih*, as we did with Canada and the Vatican. And yet in practice, old habits of thought and deference prevent even the best of us from doing so consistently on our own.

I continually experience this within all of the groups I work with. While holding to the vision of a new independent Republic based on common law, our best people will still insist on going into the lawless "crown" or de facto courts to remedy the latest injustice done against them. They cannot simply turn away from the old regime. Their psychological and energetic dependence on what is familiar runs far deeper within them than they understand, because one's position within the collective symbiosis is largely invisible to the untrained mind. In short, we are all part of a bigger and hidden "group mind" – the Bible calls it our Angel – that can only be nullified by another collective.

What this means in practice is that, regardless of anyone's degree of personal "awareness", everyone seems to be waiting in trepidation for something or someone else to make the final break and bring in a new regime. Until then, they accommodate, and worry about how to "protect" themselves and others from the present system. It is therefore hardly surprising that our membership within the Republic and common law movement has remained largely a passive and waiting one, with their eyes and feet mired in the past, waiting for someone else's leadership.

The only remedy for this immobility is provided collectively through the creation of another group identity and system into which we can draw people out of the status quo; and, by that moment when a critical mass is reached and not only consciousness but the capacity to act differently emerges among many people. This emergence is always unpredictable, but when it occurs, a huge shift across society happens almost overnight, as history amply demonstrates. And then the new *shih* alignment can become an actuality.

In many ways, all that we do today is a preparation for the opportunities created by the moment in time, that upcoming window of action, when a new and free society can come into being from the ground up. To quote Sun Tzu again,

Operations must always be geared to the rapid seizure and exploitation of the key moment of opportunity created in battle, which can never be predicted. The prime purpose of operational commanders is to recognize and act decisively upon such fleeting moments.

The operational commanders, in our case, are the on-the-ground local organizers whose job it is to build the movement in their communities by empowering wider numbers with the idea and reality that they can govern themselves according to a new and higher law, completely separate from the existing institutions.

In that regard, the convening of the Peoples' Assemblies is an expression of this long struggle to establish a new collective *shih*, because it puts flesh on the idea that fundamental change lies only in our own hands.

The Peoples' Assemblies

The Revolution may have been affected first in the hearts and minds of the People, but it took shape in our Constitutional Conventions, where the People learned how to hold and wield power for themselves. **– John Adams, 1791**

The Commons of England assembled in Parliament declare that the people under God are the origin of all just power, and have the supreme authority of the nation. Whatsoever is enacted and declared law by the Commons alone has the force of law, and all the people are included thereby, with or without the consent of the king. - **An Act to Establish the High Court of Justice, House of Commons, London, January 4, 1649**

Under this Proclamation, all lawful authority now resides in the People gathered in an elected Congress and other governmental bodies established by the People under Common Law. **– A Public Proclamation abolishing Crown Authority in Canada, January 15, 2015**

....

Our course of action is clear if the words above become part of our very thought and fiber, and gather those of us so united by this vision into permanent legislative Assemblies where we covenant to establish a new form of law and government. Such an action, replicated in many communities across Kanata, will constitute the real emergence of our Republic as it sets down its roots among the people. And then the real battle will begin.

Let us be very clear that by creating such a new authority alongside the old one – by drawing the *shih* of the old regime into our own sphere – we are entering into a state of civil war, both politically and spiritually. We are drawing a line and separating ourselves unalterably from the past by actively disestablishing the thing called Canada and crown law. The firmer our resolve and the more people we draw into our new Republic, the more peaceful will be this transition.

We can only undertake this monumental step collectively, through a new legal and political framework embodied in the Peoples' Assemblies; for as legislative bodies, it is the Assemblies that can lawfully establish the Republican common law courts and create the laws that are the skeleton of our new society.

The People are the source of all law, government and sovereign authority. This foundational Republican principle means that any group of people who covenant together under an Oath can formulate, debate and pass laws which are binding on themselves and are enforceable, and subject to no other authority except that to which they agree. The Peoples' Assemblies, once lawfully convened, are therefore wholly legitimate legislatures that are part of a new Republic. And one of the essential tasks of the Assemblies is to not only establish such a new local jurisdiction, and *shih*, but to elect delegates to a national Congress of the Republic.

People, especially Canadians, have to relearn freedom by beginning to actually practice it, and reclaiming their own *shih* autonomy. The Assemblies provide a sure way for them to do so, as matters of community concern are discussed and resolved directly in what are practical schools in self-government. When people feel the power of taking all matters into their own hands, and passing and enforcing laws in their own name, the Republic will become real as the old regime crumbles.

Conclusions

We began by observing how the present global tyranny is an energy sucking parasite whose ultimate consequence will be the eradication of life as we know it on mother earth. Our purpose, of shattering that entity and restoring natural law and life to our world, cannot be achieved without recognizing and winning back the essential energy that is drained from us through our participation in this global machinery of death. Our every thought and action must therefore be geared towards regaining this *shih* energy by establishing new courts, assemblies and communities utterly separate from the old institutions, to allow people to leave them once and for all.

Those of you readers who will be "more than hearers of the word, but doers as well", are like a sharp point of a spear constantly poised for battle. You will create the first wedge through which many others will follow, provided that you remain sharp, clear and consistent. Because you will form the blueprint of a new society, what you do today and tomorrow is of sacred importance for the future of our people. If you waver or backslide, there will be no such future.

"For you have been set apart to bind the kings of the earth, and bring to judgement the nobles, and to bring to nothing their pride and power. This is the task given to the righteous remnant, so that all may know the truth and stand within the justice of God" – Psalm 149, and cited at the trial of King Charles by the High Court of Justice of the People in Parliament, January 1649

Appendix 4: Common Law Court Documents

PUBLIC NOTICE OF CLAIM OF RIGHT made under the Common Law

Issued by _____ on _____

in the community of _____

I, _____, give public notice of my personal claim of right and of lawful excuse to convene and establish a common law court under my liberty as a flesh and blood man or woman; and I do hereby call upon the support of all competent men and women to assist me in this lawful right.

I further give public notice of my personal claim of right and of lawful excuse to convene and establish as part of such a court a jury of my peers, consisting of twelve men or women, to judge a matter affecting the well being, rights and safety of myself and my community, that matter being the following: *(Description of issue, statement of claim and parties in the claim)*

I further give public notice that this jury of my peers has the jurisdictional competence to judge this matter and issue a sentence and verdict within the said common law court based upon proven and lawful evidence presented within its court.

I hereby publicly call upon and request the support of my community to establish this common law court and its jury of twelve men or women, to be sworn to act in such a capacity for the duration of the court proceedings, according to Natural Law and the rules of evidence and due process. I make this public claim of right freely, without coercion or ulterior motive, in the interest of justice and the public welfare.

_____ **Claimant**

_____ **Witness**

_____ **Date**

NOTICE AND WARRANT TO DEPUTIZE

ISSUED UNDER THE AUTHORITY OF THE SHERIFF'S OFFICE OF THE INTERNATIONAL COMMON LAW COURT OF JUSTICE

To all Peace Officers and Law or Statute Enforcement Officials:

This Public Notice is issued to you as a lawful warrant by the Common Law Court of Justice, placing you under the jurisdiction of the Court and Natural Justice, and deputizing you as its officers.

Upon your taking the appended Oath of Common Law Court Office, you are empowered to act as the lawful agents and protectors of the Court and its proceedings, and to serve and enforce its writs, warrants, summonses and court orders on any and all persons and corporations named by the Court.

If you choose not to take this Oath of Office, you are compelled and ordered by the Court and by Natural Law to refrain from interfering with the actions of other Officers so deputized and empowered to act for the Court. **If you resist, disrupt or impede the actions of the Court or its Officers you can and will be charged with criminal assault and obstruction of justice.**

Issued on _____ in the Community of _____

by the following Agent or Sworn Peace Officer of the Common Law Court of Justice:

_____ (signed)

Authorized by the Sheriff's Office of the local
Common Law Court of Justice with the binding force of the Law

Oath of Common Law Court Office

To be issued to any sworn agent of the Court or to all persons or law enforcement officers deputized by the Court or its Sheriffs

I, _____, being of sound mind and clear conscience, do hereby swear that I will faithfully and justly execute the office of an agent of the Common Law Court of Justice according to the best of my abilities.

I understand that if I fail in my duties or if I betray the responsibilities and trust of my office I will forfeit my right to this position and will face dismissal and possible legal action.

I take this solemn oath freely, without coercion, reservation or ulterior motive, according to my conscience as a free man or woman, and as a flesh and blood man or woman and as a citizen under the authority and jurisdiction of the Common Law.

_____ (signed)

_____ (date)

Authorized by the Sheriff's Office of the local Common Law Court of Justice with the binding force of the Law

Appendix Five: ITCCS Program

What We Want: Seven Steps to Freedom
Issued by the International Tribunal of Crimes of Church and State
(ITCCS)
April 15, 2016

1. The political and legal disestablishment of the Vatican, the Roman Catholic Church, the Anglican Church, the United Church of Canada and all other churches and bodies engaged in or convicted of crimes against children and humanity.

2. The seizure of the assets and properties of these corporate church bodies and the arrest of their officers.

3. The opening and publishing of the archives and documents of these churches and the return of the remains of their victims for a proper burial.

4. The licensing of all clergy as public servants under oath to a Common Law Constitution, and their active monitoring by the citizenry.

5. The immediate arrest of all known or suspected child abusers, killers and traiffickers and those who protect them, and their trial in citizen-led common law courts of justice.

6. The establishment of permanent citizen militias and local common law courts to ensure the safety of children and communities.

7. The nullification and replacement of all governmental, religious, corporate, police and judicial bodies that commit or aid and abet crimes against children and humanity.

www.itccs.org , www.murderbydecree.com

itccsoffice@gmail.com

Appendix 6: The Art and Rules of War

(With acknowledgement to Sun Tzu and Karl von Clausewitz)

A. Core Principles

1. The sole purpose of war is the annihilation of the enemy. To aim at anything short of this invites defeat.

2. Enemies, like all opposites, are mutually dependent on one another, being part of a greater unity and purpose. Thus, enemies are defeated not by their abolition but by their absorption into that greater whole.

3. Striking at the heart of the enemy is the ultimate doctrine for victory and has no substitute. All strategy must be directed towards this purpose.

4. Purpose precedes action and must never be shaped by it. Defeat is assured when action precedes purpose. Battles are lost when purpose dissolves into random response.

5. Wars are won only when a unified leadership transforms random events into controlled outcomes, by purposely shaping such events.

6. One skilled in battle summons one's enemy and is not summoned by them; one skilled forms the ground of battle, and the enemy must follow; offers, and the enemy must take. Thus is the victorious army first victorious and then does battle, while the defeated army first does battle and then seeks victory.

7. Nothing is permanent in life except conflict and change. Therefore, nothing is permanent in war except uncertainty, the recognition of which must guide all strategy.

8. It is the nature of war that swiftness rules. Everything will be won with swift action at the key moment, or lost without it.

9. Power is found not in solid or predictable things but in the constant flow of relationships, which are always changing. The power of a squirrel to cross a river on a log lies neither in the squirrel nor the log, but in their momentary combination. That temporary combination is their power.

10. Every additional link required in the attaining of an objective causes delay, confusion and failure to increase exponentially. Every link removed from the achieving of an objective causes clarity, vigor and success to increase exponentially.

11. Knowing the enemy and knowing yourself: in every battle, no danger. Not knowing the enemy and knowing yourself: one defeat for every victory. Not knowing the enemy and not knowing yourself: in every battle, certain defeat.

12. There can be no reliable defense in war, since any defensive posture invites attack.

B. Strategy

13. Engagement with an enemy cannot be avoided. Warfare by its nature compels direct engagement. Maneuver is an unreliable means to final victory, and being a tactical consideration, is but one aspect of a command strategy.

14. Nothing will demoralize and defeat an army primed for battle quicker than avoiding a direct engagement with an enemy. Therefore, all maneuver must always be aimed at and result in such rapid engagement.

15. An army that sees fear or indecision in its commanders will collapse. Chain of command is sustained fundamentally by the valor and determined example of the commanders, and by their demonstrated capacity to grapple directly with the enemy and triumph.

16. Shock attack is preferable to stealth, since shock maximizes an army's impact as well as the fighting spirit of its troops, while restricting the enemy's options and capacity to attack.

17. To receive a blow even when prepared is to be weakened. One can only gain victory through the offensive. Defend and one is insufficient. Attack and one has a surplus.

18. Seasoned enemies expect and are trained for the unpredictable, and cannot be easily ambushed, decoyed or misled. Win victory therefore through naked force aimed at an enemy's weakest point.

19. The morale of one's troops is a key but shifting and random factor in battle, and can only be established by the strong leadership of the commanders.

20. Whoever depends on a majority for victory must reflect its weakest aspects and must thereby be defeated.

21. Seasoned minorities alone are capable of sustained and purposeful action and thereby, victory. Only veterans are capable of victorious combat, by leading the inexperienced or wavering mass in their wake. The leadership of this vanguard of veterans is the key to victory in every battle.

22. Victory is formed by the strategic command but is won by the operational commanders. The quality of these secondary leaders and their cadres is fundamental to any victory.

23. When I am few and my enemy is many, I can use the few to strike the many because those whom I battle are restricted, being larger and more unwieldy. Their strength thereby becomes their weakness.

24. The clarity and will of the commander forms the ground of the entire army; and such clarity comes from personal honesty and realism. The commander must never issue ambiguous or contradictory orders but act only from his own clarity, calmness and will.

25. Always carefully discern the enemy's purpose. The knowledge of the enemy comes only from active contact with them. Provoke them to reveal themselves, assessing their nature and responses. Prick them and know their movements. Probe them and learn their strengths and deficiencies.

26. Never reinforce error or defeat. Let your understanding move fluidly with each new experience. There is never a final or definitive outcome to the army that moves like water.

27. By being without permanent form and fluid in your movements and tactics, you compel your enemy to defend against you at every point. He is thereby dissipated and weakened, and kept ignorant of your purpose while forced to reveal his condition to you.

28. By this means of formlessness, you can force the strongest enemy to conform to the ground you have chosen for it, on the terms of your victory. But without foreknowledge of the ground itself, none of this is possible.

29. Therefore, active reconnaissance and good intelligence before any engagement are essential to victory. The commander who acts without knowing the enemy and the terrain first invites disaster.

30. Engage an enemy with what they expect, so that what you allow them to see confirms their own prejudices. This settles them into predictable patterns of response, distracting them from your actions while you wait calmly for the extraordinary moment: that which the enemy cannot anticipate or prepare for, being confirmed in their patterns.

31. Be in this manner invisible and unfathomable to your enemy. To be thus without form, first be so orthodox that nothing remains to give you away. Then be so extraordinary that no-one can predict your action or purpose. Use the extraordinary to win victory.

32. Ride the inadequacies of your enemy. Go by unpredicted ways. Attack where your enemy has not taken precautions and avoid where they have.

33. Find your own army to you with deeds. Do not command them with words.

C. Tactics-Operations

34. Successful tactics are the offspring of true experience but must always remain supple and expendable. Tactics are by their nature transitory; if they become enshrined into a permanent strategy or doctrine, they are a recipe for disaster.

35. Operations must always be geared to the rapid seizure and exploitation of the key moment of opportunity created in battle, which can never be predicted. The prime purpose of operational commanders is to recognize and act decisively upon such fleeting moments.

36. An unshakeable will to pursue victory using every opportunity is the one essential quality of tactical commanders, and tends to overcome every setback or unforeseen event.

37. Before engaging an enemy, form the ground of battle on terms favourable to you, then shape the ground to deceive the enemy, with actions that fit the enemy's own mind and situation. Thus you form victory before and during battle by always standing on your own ground.

38. Never repeat successful tactics or maneuvers with the same enemy, or they will recover and adapt to your tactics.

39. Do not respond to the ground your enemy has prepared for you, but instead, shape their ground. Then they have no alternative but to be led by you, as if it was their own idea. This is skill.

40. Hide the time of battle from an enemy, and make what he loves and defends your first objective. When near, manifest far; when able, manifest inability, so as to confuse him.

41. Let your plans be as dark as night, then strike like a thunderbolt with utter surprise. Prior to such an attack, feign weakness and offer the enemy a truce, to lull his defences. The unexpected attack always negates the superior strength of an enemy.
42. Respond to aggression by creating space so as to control the actions of the aggressor. Resist and you swell the attacker. Create room for the aggressor and he will dissipate.

43. When aggression by a superior foe remains undissipated despite your actions, engage the aggression by guiding it into conditions favorable to you. Feign retreat to draw his forces into traps.

44. Use order to await chaos, stillness to await clamor. At the right moment, not acting is the most skillful action.

45. Hostile ground heightens your focus. Cut off from home support, you take nourishment from the enemy and learn self-reliance. Such supply lines cannot be severed. Use the threat surrounding you to stay united and inspire your army.

46. Place your soldiers where they cannot leave, and have no alternative but to fight or die. Facing death, they find their true strength and cannot be routed. When they cannot leave, they stand firm and fight. For thus do extreme situations cause your troops to find a deeper resolve and a source of inner power.

47. This deeper resolve cannot be taught or accomplished by training or commands. Dire circumstances automatically evoke it, unsought yet attained. Commanders must fashion these moments by using hopeless situations to their advantage. The right relationships, especially when facing disaster, unleash enormous power greater than the individual parts.

48. If a mightier enemy pauses though enjoying an advantage, they are tired. If divisions appear in their ranks, they are frightened. If their commander repeatedly speaks soothing reassurances to his army, he has lost his power. Many punishments indicate panic. Many bribes and rewards mean the enemy is seeking retreat.

49. Do not confront the enemy in their strength but at the points of their weakness, which are in constant flux. They must be recognized and attacked swiftly.

50. In all engagements, aim at and seize something the enemy holds dear; then their strength and plans are rendered useless, and they must stop and respond on your terms. Likewise, whatever you love makes you vulnerable and prone to manipulation: prepare yourself to relinquish it.

Addendum: The Nature of Rear Guard Actions

I. Rear guard actions are required when an army is in retreat or maneuver and seeks to decoy an enemy by camouflaging its movements or weaknesses with a deceptive appearance of strength or initiative.

II. A rear guard action is inherently defensive and arises from either desperation or weakness. An army advancing from strength has no need of rear guard measures. Only an army on the strategic defensive must screen its real aims and movements.

III. When an enemy detaches a portion of its army as a rear guard force, one must respond quickly and aggressively against the enemy since he is off balance and vulnerable. Yet one must never respond on the terms of an enemy's read guard force, which is merely a delaying decoy, but rather must push past such a force in order to strike at the main body of the enemy that is in retreat or maneuver.

IV. Rear guard actions are temporary stop gap measures and are often improvised under desperate conditions, and thus cannot be relied upon to restrain for long an enemy's main body. Rear guard actions are accordingly a means of last resort, and since they will be recognized as such by a sage adversary, employing such a measure can invoke an undesired retaliatory response by an enemy that may render the rear guard ineffective and self-defeating.

V. For these reasons, rear guard actions must be employed very selectively and judiciously. By themselves they can never secure victory. They must be launched only in conjunction with a broader offensive strategy that seeks to overcome one's enemy not through deception and maneuver but by a redeployment that shifts the *shih* and strategic initiative to one's own army.

Appendix 7:

Biography of Rev. Kevin Daniel Annett M.A., M.Div.

Nobel Peace Prize Nominee (2014, 2015); Recipient of the Prague Peace Award (2016); Community minister, human rights consultant and Special Adviser to the International Tribunal of Crimes of Church and State (ITCCS). Award winning film maker, lecturer, broadcaster and author*. Born 1956, Edmonton, Canada.

Education

B.A. (Anthropology), University of British Columbia (UBC), 1983; M.A. (Political Science), UBC 1986; M.Div. (Master of Divinity), Vancouver School of Theology, 1990.

Ordained as a clergyman in the United Church of Canada, 1990; held three pastoral positions, including at St. Andrew's United Church, Port Alberni, BC, 1992-1995. Fired from there without cause and expelled from the ministry without due process, 1995-97, after publicly exposing the murder of aboriginal children and theft of native land by the United Church of Canada.

Organized the first public inquiry into crimes in Canadian Indian residential schools, June 12-14, 1998 in Vancouver (co-sponsored by the United Nations affiliate IHRAAM). Established the first permanent body to further this inquiry: The Truth Commission into Genocide in Canada, September 2000. Published the first account of genocidal crimes in Indian residential schools: *Hidden from History: The Canadian Holocaust* (March 2001).

Formed The Friends and Relatives of the Disappeared (FRD) in Vancouver and Toronto, 2005-2010; led high profile church occupations and national conferences into missing residential school children. Forced Canadian government's "official apology" for Indian residential schools, June 8, 2008.

Led public protests and exorcism ceremonies at the Vatican, 2009-2010; won the endorsement of the Italian Democratic and Radical parties and the

Municipality of Genoa for an international inquiry into crimes of Genocide in Canada, April 2010.

Co-founded the International Tribunal of Crimes of Church and State (ITCCS) in Dublin, June 15, 2010; appointed ITCCS North American Field Secretary.

Served as Chief Adviser to the International Common Law Court of Justice in Brussels in its two criminal cases against the Vatican, the Crown of England and Canada and its churches for Crimes against Humanity, 2012-14. Forced the resignation from his office of Pope Benedict, Joseph Ratzinger, in February 2013 after his conviction in the Common Law Court, along with Cardinals Bertone, Brady and Jesuit leader Adolfo Pachon.

As Adviser to the Provisional Council of the Republic of Kanata, helped establish its founding Proclamation and Constitution in Winnipeg, January 15, 2015. Serves as one of three chief conveners for the Republic. Launched and hosts the Republic's media arm Radio Free Kanata. *(www.bbsradio.com/radiofreekanata)*

Presently serves as spiritual adviser and elder to the Covenant of Free Congregational Christians (The Covenanters).

*Publications and Films

Books:

Establishing the Reign of Natural Liberty: A Common Law Training Manual (Amazon, March 2017)

Murder by Decree: The Crime of Genocide in Canada - A Counter Report to the Truth and Reconciliation Commission (Amazon, 2016. See www.murderbydecree.com)

Unrelenting: Between Sodom and Zion (Amazon, 2016)

Truth Tellers' Shield: A Whistleblowers Manual (Amazon, 2016)

1497 and so on: A History of White People in Canada (Amazon, November 2016)

Samuel Wedge: Memoirs of Necropolis (Author House, 2015)

Unrepentant: Disrobing the Emperor (O Books, 2010)

Hidden No Longer: Genocide in Canada, Past and Present (2010, self published)

Love and Death in the Valley (First Books, 2001)

Hidden from History: The Canadian Holocaust (2001, self published)
Film:

Unrepentant: Kevin Annett and Canada's Genocide (2006) - Winnier of Best Documentary at the New York Independent Film Festival (2006) and the Los Angeles Independent Film Festival (2007); Best Film, Creation Aboriginal Film Festival, Edmonton (2009)

See also an insightful personal interview "Who is Kevin Annett?" (2013) at: https://www.youtube.com/watch?v=AY4h3hDjOYM

Websites and Contact:

www.itccs.org , www.murderbydecree.com , www.KevinAnnett.com

Email addresses: hiddenfromhistory1@gmail.com , thecommonland@gmail.com

Leave phone messages for Kevin Annett at 386-323-5774 (USA).

Kevin and others outside the Canadian Embassy, London, England - April 2010

Sources and Resources

On the nature and historical roots of the Common Law see these source books and their varying interpretations:

Bouvier's Law Dictionary by John Bouvier, (1856) *Legal Maxims* by Broom and Bouvier, (1856) *A Dictionary of Law* by William C. Anderson, (1893) *Black's Law Dictionary* by Henry Campell Black, (3rd, 4th, 5th, and 6th Editions, 1933-1990) *Maxims of Law* by Charles A. Weisman, (1990); *The Tyrannicide Brief* by Geoffrey Robertson (2005).

See also Judge Oliver Wendell Holmes, *The Common Law* (1881); T. F. Plucknett, *Concise History of the Common Law* (5th ed. 1956); H. Potter, *Historical Introduction to English Law and Its Institutions* (4th ed. 1958); A. R. Hogue, *Origins of the Common Law* (1966); R. C. van Caenegem, *The Birth of the English Common Law* (1973); J. H. Baker, *The Legal Profession and the Common Law* (1986); *The Common Law World* by Able and Lewis (1988).

On the application of Common Law to crimes against humanity in Canada see:

Murder by Decree: The Crime of Genocide in Canada, Past and Present – A Counter-Report to the 'Truth and Reconciliation Commission' by Kevin D. Annett (www.amazon.com, 2016) (www.murderbydecree.com)

The Case of the Pope by Geoffrey Robertson (2010)
https://www.amazon.ca/Case-Pope-Geoffrey-Robertson/dp/0241953847

"The Common Law Court of Justice will provide speakers and training programs for anyone interested in implementing the vision and actions described in this Manual. For more information write to itccsoffice@gmail.com.

The Meaning of Magna Carta

Magna Carta, the "Great Charter" that first defined the rights of Englishmen and restricted the power of monarchy, was published in 1215 after local barons held a figurative and literal knife to the throat of King John, who ratified it. The Charter did not grant rights to anyone but simply recognized pre-existing natural liberties that the English had enjoyed long before the Normans conquered their island in 1066. Nevertheless, Magna Carta has been the basis of much of the body of law upholding our inherent rights and freedoms, like the ones enunciated in Paragraphs 38-40 of the Charter:

In future no official shall place a man on trial upon his own unsupported statement, without producing credible witnesses to the truth of it.

No free man shall be seized or imprisoned, or stripped of his rights or possessions, or outlawed or exiled, or deprived of his standing in any way, nor will we proceed with force against him, or send others to do so, except by the lawful judgment of his equals or by the law of the land.

To no one will we sell, to no one deny or delay right or justice.

Not surprisingly, kings and popes continually tried to nullify and ignore Magna Carta because of its attempt to restrict their power and uphold the sovereignty of the people. Shortly after the Charter's promulgation, Pope Innocent III issued a papal bull "annulling" it and threatening with excommunication King John and all those who'd signed it.
(http://www.concordatwatch.eu/showtopic.php?org_id=889&kb_header_id=41481)

Regardless, the Great Charter was reissued several times over the centuries and played a pivotal role in the rise of the English parliament and the Commons as a self-governing body. It also was foundational in the establishment of the United States Constitution and every international human rights convention since then. The arcane and historically-specific provisions of much of the Charter does not distract from its continued ability to act as a counterweight against tyranny and arbitrary power.

The Full-text translation of the 1215 edition of Magna Carta:

Clauses marked (+) are still valid under the charter of 1225, but with a few minor amendments. Clauses marked (*) were omitted in all later reissues of the charter. In the charter itself the clauses are not numbered, and the text reads continuously. The translation sets out to convey the sense rather than the precise wording of the original Latin. **Darkened sections are especially relevant to common law rights.**

JOHN, by the grace of God King of England, Lord of Ireland, Duke of Normandy and Aquitaine, and Count of Anjou, to his archbishops, bishops, abbots, earls, barons, justices, foresters, sheriffs, stewards, servants, and to all his officials and loyal subjects, Greeting. KNOW THAT BEFORE GOD, for the health of our soul and those of our ancestors and heirs, to the honour of God, the exaltation of the holy Church, and the better ordering of our kingdom, at the advice of our reverend fathers Stephen, archbishop of Canterbury, primate of all England, and cardinal of the holy Roman Church, Henry archbishop of Dublin, William bishop of London, Peter bishop of Winchester, Jocelin bishop of Bath and Glastonbury, Hugh bishop of Lincoln, Walter bishop of Worcester, William bishop of Coventry, Benedict bishop of Rochester, Master Pandulf subdeacon and member of the papal household, Brother Aymeric master of the knighthood of the Temple in England, William Marshal earl of Pembroke, William earl of Salisbury, William earl of Warren, William earl of Arundel, Alan of Galloway constable of Scotland, Warin fitz Gerald, Peter fitz Herbert, Hubert de Burgh seneschal of Poitou, Hugh de Neville, Matthew fitz Herbert, Thomas Basset, Alan Basset, Philip Daubeny, Robert de Roppeley, John Marshal, John fitz Hugh, and other loyal subjects:

+ (1) FIRST, THAT WE HAVE GRANTED TO GOD, and by this present charter have confirmed for us and our heirs in perpetuity, that the English Church shall be free, and shall have its rights undiminished, and its liberties unimpaired. That we wish this so to be observed, appears from the fact that of our own free will, before the outbreak of the present dispute between us and our barons, we granted and confirmed by charter the freedom of the Church's elections - a right reckoned to be of the greatest necessity and importance to it - and caused this to be confirmed by Pope Innocent III. This freedom we shall observe ourselves, and desire to be observed in good faith by our heirs in perpetuity.

TO ALL FREE MEN OF OUR KINGDOM we have also granted, for us and our heirs for ever, all the liberties written out below, to have and to keep for them and their heirs, of us and our heirs:

(2) If any earl, baron, or other person that holds lands directly of the Crown, for military service, shall die, and at his death his heir shall be of full age and owe a 'relief', the heir shall have his inheritance on payment of the ancient scale of 'relief'. That is to say, the heir or heirs of an earl shall pay £100 for the entire earl's barony, the heir or heirs of a knight 100s. at most for the entire knight's 'fee', and any man that owes less shall pay less, in accordance with the ancient

usage of 'fees'.

(3) But if the heir of such a person is under age and a ward, when he comes of age he shall have his inheritance without 'relief' or fine.

(4) The guardian of the land of an heir who is under age shall take from it only reasonable revenues, customary dues, and feudal services. He shall do this without destruction or damage to men or property. If we have given the guardianship of the land to a sheriff, or to any person answerable to us for the revenues, and he commits destruction or damage, we will exact compensation from him, and the land shall be entrusted to two worthy and prudent men of the same 'fee', who shall be answerable to us for the revenues, or to the person to whom we have assigned them. If we have given or sold to anyone the guardianship of such land, and he causes destruction or damage, he shall lose the guardianship of it, and it shall be handed over to two worthy and prudent men of the same 'fee', who shall be similarly answerable to us.

(5) For so long as a guardian has guardianship of such land, he shall maintain the houses, parks, fish preserves, ponds, mills, and everything else pertaining to it, from the revenues of the land itself. When the heir comes of age, he shall restore the whole land to him, stocked with plough teams and such implements of husbandry as the season demands and the revenues from the land can reasonably bear.

(6) Heirs may be given in marriage, but not to someone of lower social standing. Before a marriage takes place, it shall be made known to the heir's next-of-kin.

(7) At her husband's death, a widow may have her marriage portion and inheritance at once and without trouble. She shall pay nothing

for her dower, marriage portion, or any inheritance that she and her husband held jointly on the day of his death. She may remain in her husband's house for forty days after his death, and within this period her dower shall be assigned to her.

(8) No widow shall be compelled to marry, so long as she wishes to remain without a husband. But she must give security that she will not marry without royal consent, if she holds her lands of the Crown, or without the consent of whatever other lord she may hold them of.

(9) Neither we nor our officials will seize any land or rent in payment of a debt, so long as the debtor has movable goods sufficient to discharge the debt. A debtor's sureties shall not be distrained upon so long as the debtor himself can discharge his debt. If, for lack of means, the debtor is unable to discharge his debt, his sureties shall be answerable for it. If they so desire, they may have the debtor's lands and rents until they have received satisfaction for the debt that they paid for him, unless the debtor can show that he has settled his obligations to them.

* (10) If anyone who has borrowed a sum of money from Jews dies before the debt has been repaid, his heir shall pay no interest on the debt for so long as he remains under age, irrespective of whom he holds his lands. If such a debt falls into the hands of the Crown, it will take nothing except the principal sum specified in the bond.

* (11) If a man dies owing money to Jews, his wife may have her dower and pay nothing towards the debt from it. If he leaves children that are under age, their needs may also be provided for on a scale appropriate to the size of his holding of lands. The debt is to be paid out of the residue, reserving the service due to his feudal lords. Debts owed to persons other than Jews are to be dealt with similarly.

* (12) No 'scutage' or 'aid' may be levied in our kingdom without its general consent, unless it is for the ransom of our person, to make our eldest son a knight, and (once) to marry our eldest daughter. For these purposes only a reasonable 'aid' may be levied. 'Aids' from the city of London are to be treated similarly.

+ **(13) The city of London shall enjoy all its ancient liberties and free customs, both by land and by water. We also will and grant that all other cities, boroughs, towns, and ports shall enjoy all their liberties and free customs.**

* (14) To obtain the general consent of the realm for the assessment of an 'aid' - except in the three cases specified above - or a 'scutage', we will cause the archbishops, bishops, abbots, earls, and greater barons to be summoned individually by letter. To those who hold lands directly of us we will cause a general summons to be issued, through the sheriffs and other officials, to come together on a fixed day (of which at least forty days notice shall be given) and at a fixed place. In all letters of summons, the cause of the summons will be stated. When a summons has been issued, the business appointed for the day shall go forward in accordance with the resolution of those present, even if not all those who were summoned have appeared.

* (15) In future we will allow no one to levy an 'aid' from his free men, except to ransom his person, to make his eldest son a knight, and (once) to marry his eldest daughter. For these purposes only a reasonable 'aid' may be levied.

(16) No man shall be forced to perform more service for a knight's 'fee', or other free holding of land, than is due from it.

(17) Ordinary lawsuits shall not follow the royal court around, but shall be held in a fixed place.

(18) Inquests of novel disseisin, mort d'ancestor, and darrein presentment shall be taken only in their proper county court. We ourselves, or in our absence abroad our chief justice, will send two justices to each county four times a year, and these justices, with four knights of the county elected by the county itself, shall hold the assizes in the county court, on the day and in the place where the court meets.

(19) If any assizes cannot be taken on the day of the county court, as many knights and freeholders shall afterwards remain behind, of those who have attended the court, as will suffice for the administration of justice, having regard to the volume of business to be done.

(20) For a trivial offence, a free man shall be fined only in proportion to the degree of his offence, and for a serious offence correspondingly, but not so heavily as to deprive him of his livelihood. In the same way, a merchant shall be spared his merchandise, and a villein the implements of his husbandry, if they fall upon the mercy of a royal court. None of these fines shall be imposed except by the assessment on oath of reputable men of the neighbourhood.

(21) Earls and barons shall be fined only by their equals, and in proportion to the gravity of their offence.

(22) A fine imposed upon the lay property of a clerk in holy orders shall be assessed upon the same principles, without reference to the value of his ecclesiastical benefice.

(23) No town or person shall be forced to build bridges over rivers

except those with an ancient obligation to do so.

(24) No sheriff, constable, coroners, or other royal officials are to hold lawsuits that should be held by the royal justices.

* (25) Every county, hundred, wapentake, and tithing shall remain at its ancient rent, without increase, except the royal demesne manors.

(26) If at the death of a man who holds a lay 'fee' of the Crown, a sheriff or royal official produces royal letters patent of summons for a debt due to the Crown, it shall be lawful for them to seize and list movable goods found in the lay 'fee' of the dead man to the value of the debt, as assessed by worthy men. Nothing shall be removed until the whole debt is paid, when the residue shall be given over to the executors to carry out the dead man's will. If no debt is due to the Crown, all the movable goods shall be regarded as the property of the dead man, except the reasonable shares of his wife and children.

* (27) If a free man dies intestate, his movable goods are to be distributed by his next-of-kin and friends, under the supervision of the Church. The rights of his debtors are to be preserved.

(28) No constable or other royal official shall take corn or other movable goods from any man without immediate payment, unless the seller voluntarily offers postponement of this.

(29) No constable may compel a knight to pay money for castle-guard if the knight is willing to undertake the guard in person, or with reasonable excuse to supply some other fit man to do it. A knight taken or sent on military service shall be excused from castle-guard for the period of this service.

(30) No sheriff, royal official, or other person shall take horses or carts for transport from any free man, without his consent.

(31) Neither we nor any royal official will take wood for our castle, or for any other purpose, without the consent of the owner.

(32) We will not keep the lands of people convicted of felony in our hand for longer than a year and a day, after which they shall be returned to the lords of the 'fees' concerned.

(33) All fish-weirs shall be removed from the Thames, the Medway, and throughout the whole of England, except on the sea coast.

(34) The writ called precipe shall not in future be issued to anyone in respect of any holding of land, if a free man could thereby be deprived of the right of trial in his own lord's court.

(35) There shall be standard measures of wine, ale, and corn (the London quarter), throughout the kingdom. There shall also be a standard width of dyed cloth, russet, and haberject, namely two ells within the selvedges.

(36) In future nothing shall be paid or accepted for the issue of a writ of inquisition of life or limbs. It shall be given gratis, and not refused.

(37) If a man holds land of the Crown by 'fee-farm', 'socage', or 'burgage', and also holds land of someone else for knight's service, we will not have guardianship of his heir, nor of the land that belongs to the other person's 'fee', by virtue of the 'fee-farm', 'socage', or 'burgage', unless the 'fee-farm' owes knight's service. We will not have the guardianship of a man's heir, or of land that he holds of someone else, by reason of any small property that he may hold of the Crown for a service of knives, arrows, or the like.

(38) In future no official shall place a man on trial upon his own unsupported statement, without producing credible witnesses to the truth of it.

+ (39) No free man shall be seized or imprisoned, or stripped of his rights or possessions, or outlawed or exiled, or deprived of his standing in any way, nor will we proceed with force against him, or send others to do so, except by the lawful judgment of his equals or by the law of the land.

+ (40) To no one will we sell, to no one deny or delay right or justice.

(41) All merchants may enter or leave England unharmed and without fear, and may stay or travel within it, by land or water, for purposes of trade, free from all illegal exactions, in accordance with ancient and lawful customs. This, however, does not apply in time of war to merchants from a country that is at war with us. Any such merchants found in our country at the outbreak of war shall be detained without injury to their persons or property, until we or our chief justice have discovered how our own merchants are being treated in the country at war with us. If our own merchants are safe they shall be safe too.

* (42) In future it shall be lawful for any man to leave and return to our kingdom unharmed and without fear, by land or water, preserving his allegiance to us, except in time of war, for some short period, for the common benefit of the realm. People that have been imprisoned or outlawed in accordance with the law of the land, people from a country that is at war with us, and merchants - who shall be dealt with as stated above - are excepted from this provision.

(43) If a man holds lands of any 'escheat' such as the 'honour' of Wallingford, Nottingham, Boulogne, Lancaster, or of other 'escheats' in our hand that are baronies, at his death his heir shall give us only the 'relief' and service that he would have made to the baron, had the barony been in the baron's hand. We will hold the 'escheat' in the same manner as the baron held it.

(44) People who live outside the forest need not in future appear before the royal justices of the forest in answer to general summonses, unless they are actually involved in proceedings or are sureties for someone who has been seized for a forest offence.

* (45) We will appoint as justices, constables, sheriffs, or other officials, only men that know the law of the realm and are minded to keep it well.

(46) All barons who have founded abbeys, and have charters of English kings or ancient tenure as evidence of this, may have guardianship of them when there is no abbot, as is their due.

(47) All forests that have been created in our reign shall at once be disafforested. River-banks that have been enclosed in our reign shall be treated similarly.

*(48) All evil customs relating to forests and warrens, foresters, warreners, sheriffs and their servants, or river-banks and their wardens, are at once to be investigated in every county by twelve sworn knights of the county, and within forty days of their enquiry the evil customs are to be abolished completely and irrevocably. But we, or our chief justice if we are not in England, are first to be informed.

* (49) We will at once return all hostages and charters delivered up to us by Englishmen as security for peace or for loyal service.

* (50) We will remove completely from their offices the kinsmen of Gerard de Athée, and in future they shall hold no offices in England. The people in question are Engelard de Cigogné, Peter, Guy, and Andrew de Chanceaux, Guy de Cigogné, Geoffrey de Martigny and his brothers, Philip Marc and his brothers, with Geoffrey his nephew, and all their followers.

* (51) As soon as peace is restored, we will remove from the kingdom all the foreign knights, bowmen, their attendants, and the mercenaries that have come to it, to its harm, with horses and arms.

* (52) To any man whom we have deprived or dispossessed of lands, castles, liberties, or rights, without the lawful judgment of his equals, we will at once restore these. In cases of dispute the matter shall be resolved by the judgment of the twenty-five barons referred to below in the clause for securing the peace (§61). In cases, however, where a man was deprived or dispossessed of something without the lawful judgment of his equals by our father King Henry or our brother King Richard, and it remains in our hands or is held by others under our warranty, we shall have respite for the period commonly allowed to Crusaders, unless a lawsuit had been begun, or an enquiry had been made at our order, before we took the Cross as a Crusader. On our return from the Crusade, or if we abandon it, we will at once render justice in full.

* (53) We shall have similar respite in rendering justice in connexion with forests that are to be disafforested, or to remain forests, when these were first afforested by our father Henry or our brother Richard; with the guardianship of lands in another person's 'fee', when we have hitherto had this by virtue of a 'fee' held of us for knight's service by a third party; and with abbeys founded in another person's 'fee', in which the lord of the 'fee' claims to own a

right. On our return from the Crusade, or if we abandon it, we will at once do full justice to complaints about these matters.

(54) No one shall be arrested or imprisoned on the appeal of a woman for the death of any person except her husband.

* (55) All fines that have been given to us unjustly and against the law of the land, and all fines that we have exacted unjustly, shall be entirely remitted or the matter decided by a majority judgment of the twenty-five barons referred to below in the clause for securing the peace (§61) together with Stephen, archbishop of Canterbury, if he can be present, and such others as he wishes to bring with him. If the archbishop cannot be present, proceedings shall continue without him, provided that if any of the twenty-five barons has been involved in a similar suit himself, his judgment shall be set aside, and someone else chosen and sworn in his place, as a substitute for the single occasion, by the rest of the twenty-five.

(56) If we have deprived or dispossessed any Welshmen of land, liberties, or anything else in England or in Wales, without the lawful judgment of their equals, these are at once to be returned to them. A dispute on this point shall be determined in the Marches by the judgment of equals. English law shall apply to holdings of land in England, Welsh law to those in Wales, and the law of the Marches to those in the Marches. The Welsh shall treat us and ours in the same way.

* (57) In cases where a Welshman was deprived or dispossessed of anything, without the lawful judgment of his equals, by our father King Henry or our brother King Richard, and it remains in our hands or is held by others under our warranty, we shall have respite for the period commonly allowed to Crusaders, unless a lawsuit had been begun, or an enquiry had been made at our order, before we took

the Cross as a Crusader. But on our return from the Crusade, or if we abandon it, we will at once do full justice according to the laws of Wales and the said regions.

* (58) We will at once return the son of Llywelyn, all Welsh hostages, and the charters delive red to us as security for the peace.

* (59) With regard to the return of the sisters and hostages of Alexander, king of Scotland, his liberties and his rights, we will treat him in the same way as our other barons of England, unless it appears from the charters that we hold from his father William, formerly king of Scotland, that he should be treated otherwise. This matter shall be resolved by the judgment of his equals in our court.

(60) All these customs and liberties that we have granted shall be observed in our kingdom in so far as concerns our own relations with our subjects. Let all men of our kingdom, whether clergy or laymen, observe them similarly in their relations with their own men.

* (61) SINCE WE HAVE GRANTED ALL THESE THINGS for God, for the better ordering of our kingdom, and to allay the discord that has arisen between us and our barons, and since we desire that they shall be enjoyed in their entirety, with lasting strength, for ever, we give and grant to the barons the following security:

The barons shall elect twenty-five of their number to keep, and cause to be observed with all their might, the peace and liberties granted and confirmed to them by this charter.

If we, our chief justice, our officials, or any of our servants offend in any respect against any man, or transgress any of the articles of the peace or of this security, and the offence is made known to four of the said twenty-five barons, they shall come to us - or in our absence from the kingdom to the chief justice - to declare it and claim immediate redress.

If we, or in our absence abroad the chief justice, make no redress within forty days, reckoning from the day on which the offence was declared to us or to him, the four barons shall refer the matter to the rest of the twenty-five barons, who may distrain upon and assail us in every way possible, with the support of the whole community of the land, by seizing our castles, lands, possessions, or anything else saving only our own person and those of the queen and our children, until they have secured such redress as they have determined upon. Having secured the redress, they may then resume their normal obedience to us.

Any man who so desires may take an oath to obey the commands of the twenty-five barons for the achievement of these ends, and to join with them in assailing us to the utmost of his power. We give public and free permission to take this oath to any man who so desires, and at no time will we prohibit any man from taking it. Indeed, we will compel any of our subjects who are unwilling to take it to swear it at our command.

If one of the twenty-five barons dies or leaves the country, or is prevented in any other way from discharging his duties, the rest of them shall choose another baron in his place, at their discretion, who shall be duly sworn in as they were.

In the event of disagreement among the twenty-five barons on any matter referred to them for decision, the verdict of the majority present shall have the same validity as a unanimous verdict of the whole twenty-five, whether these were all present or some of those summoned were unwilling or unable to appear.

The twenty-five barons shall swear to obey all the above articles faithfully, and shall cause them to be obeyed by others to the best of their power.

We will not seek to procure from anyone, either by our own efforts or those of a third party, anything by which any part of these concessions or liberties might be revoked or diminished. Should such a thing be procured, it shall be null and void and we will at no time make use of it, either ourselves or through a third party.

* (62) We have remitted and pardoned fully to all men any ill-will, hurt, or grudges that have arisen between us and our subjects, whether clergy or laymen, since the beginning of the dispute. We have in addition remitted fully, and for our own part have also pardoned, to all clergy and laymen any offences committed as a result of the said dispute between Easter in the sixteenth year of our reign (i.e. 1215) and the restoration of peace.

In addition we have caused letters patent to be made for the barons, bearing witness to this security and to the concessions set out above, over the seals of Stephen archbishop of Canterbury, Henry archbishop of Dublin, the other bishops named above, and Master Pandulf.

* (63) IT IS ACCORDINGLY OUR WISH AND COMMAND that the English Church shall be free, and that men in our kingdom shall have and keep all these liberties, rights, and concessions, well and peaceably in their fullness and entirety for them and their heirs, of us and our heirs, in all things and all places for ever.

Both we and the barons have sworn that all this shall be observed in good faith and without deceit. Witness the above mentioned people and many others.

Given by our hand in the meadow that is called Runnymede, between Windsor and Staines, on the fifteenth day of June in the seventeenth year of our reign (i.e. 1215: the new regnal year began on 28 May).

103

Post script

Further publications of the International Common Law Court of Justice and its procedures and principles will be forthcoming, issued by the ICLCJ Legal Advisory Board. For additional copies of this Common Law Court Manual, write to itccsoffice@gmail.com. Payment for these copies can be made through the ITCCS paypal system at www.itccs.org.

Copyright for this Manual is held by The International Common Law Court of Justice.

Permission is granted to reproduce, use and quote from this Manual in whole or in part for strictly non-commercial purposes.

There is but one law for all, namely that law which governs all law, the Law of our Creator, the law of humanity, justice and equity. That is the law of Nature and of Nations.

– Edmund Burke, 1780

Made in United States
North Haven, CT
20 November 2022

26984923R00059